Polygon Affair

So Easy You'll Fall in Love

Gyleen X. Fitzgerald

Gyleen X. Fitzgerald

Polygon Affair

FPI Publishing

P.O. Box 247
Havre de Grace, MD 21078

www.ColourfulStitches.com

Copyright © 2013 by FPI Publishing, Inc. All rights reserved. Printed by the Anderson International Printing Group. This book may not be reproduced in whole or in part, in any form or by any means, electronic or mechanical, including photocopying, recording, or by any information storage and retrieval system now known or hereafter invented, without written permission from the publisher except in the case of reprints in the context of reviews.

The Polygon® and Butterfly Seam® logos are trademarks of Colourful Stitches, LLC and/or its subsidiaries and/or affiliates in the USA and may not be used without express written permission.

Book Design: Brian Boehm
Cover Design: Brian Boehm
Pattern Layout: Jean Ann Wright
Editor: Jean Ann Wright
Photography: Michael McCarthy
Studio Photography: Raymond C. H. McGowan
Photo Stylist: Kim Little
Copy Editor: Barbara Polston

ISBN: 978-0-9768215-6-4

LIBRARY OF CONGRESS CONTROL NUMBER: 2013951309

Dedication

To Ray, the light in my life, my love and soulmate.

Preface

My love story began when I found myself single after 27 years of marriage. My world was turned upside down and I had to "get a grip." My happy space is my quilt studio, I find solace there; it prevents me from going down the rabbit hole. In my studio, I pondered what I knew for sure…geometry and quilting. I played with shapes, moving them from left to right, cutting fabric to make pretty pictures.

Then I got serious. My passion was growing into obsession. I needed tools to improve my cutting accuracy and a technique to increase the speed of stitching. As my hands worked, my mind had time to focus on where my life had been and where it was going. You see, I'm built for love; it's a defining ingredient of my soul. Yet, I found myself without a mate. My next question was, how was he going to find me or me find him if I stayed in my studio? I had to be ready with a list of all the qualities I needed in a soulmate. I grabbed my pen.

As I completed Nightfall and Sunrise, I started and finished the Engaged quilt. I just had the feeling the time was near. Okay, yes, everyone thought I was losing my mind. I asked in workshops and lectures and pals over dinner if anyone knew this man from my list. Then, one beautiful, sunny afternoon in December, as I was leaving the post office, I stopped to chat with a neighbor, Melanie. She asked me if I was dating. Always open to possibilities, I shared my list.

"I know him," she said. "His name is Ray, my best friend."

That following Friday, I met Ray. No bells or whistles, just a nice, animated man who has traveled the world and was a foodie.

We went out…that was nice. We chatted about topics that were way too technical and geekie. He can't be the one for me, I thought. Little did I know, I was falling in love with his huge "Cookie Monster" smile. A dash of time and a few dates later, I mentioned that I don't date or better said, don't have time to date and quilt. I'm only interested in dating if it will lead to marriage. Remember, I'm the marrying type. Ray was not daunted and, after what I think was our fourth date, he asked me to marry him. I said, "Absolutely!"

Those five months, from meeting to marriage, were a blur of happiness. For the first time, I have all phases of my life in focus.

Polygon Affair, a love affair…from the geometry in the quilts that stitch our lives together to soulmates on the happiest day of life; I hope you engage in the journey reflecting on your passion and the magic of being in love.

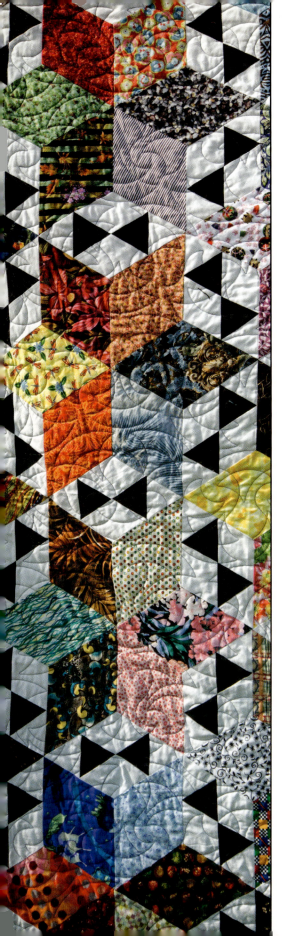

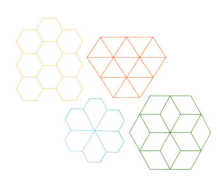

TABLE OF CONTENTS

Foreword	8
Introduction	9
Love at First Sight	10
Seeing is Believing	31
Single & Loving It	37
First Date	45
Meet & Greet Friends	55
Engaged	65
Bridesmaids' Ball	77
Bachelor Party	85
The Mother's Dance	91
Father of the Bride	99
Happily Ever After	107
Endless Love	119
Young Love…Brian's Story	122
Love Eternal…Keziah's Diary	123
Resources	124
Acknowledgments	125
About the Author	127

Foreword

I first met Gyleen in Pittsburg, Pennsylvania during Spring Market some ten years ago. I remember it clearly, the "newbie" hanging at the back of my lecture waiting to chat with me. I saw something then that has come into the light now; she is a dynamo with endless creative energy. I watched her career blossom over the years. When she contacted me about writing the foreword for Polygon Affair, I was delighted.

As I listened to her concept, I saw Gyleen "glow" when she talked about her love of geometry, love of quiltmaking, and love of life itself.

My first impression of the quilts for Polygon Affair, was wow, Gyleen has transferred all that energy and has gone big, bold, and complex. The star, hexagon, strippy, and tumbling block designs followed a contemporary style that changes scale on a whim. I should have known since Gyleen is all about the math and making things easy. When visiting as guest on *The Quilt Show*, she taught me how to do the Butterfly Seam. Her revolutionary technique opens the door to all the geometric designs in Polygon Affair requiring the notorious "Y" seam.

Polygon Affair, a love affair, I knew there was more to this story. Yes, indeed, she was in love! Polygon Affair captures this tale of true love that grows with each quilt design. Gyleen, in marital bliss, is on fire!

Alex Anderson
FOUNDING PARTNER
The Quilt Show and *Quilt Life Magazine*

Introduction

My heart flutters with excitement of new love.

I can't stop sketching, stitching, and spreading pure joy and it all started by playing with polygons. Pyramids, diamonds, cones, and hexagons are shaping my thinking of what is possible.

I am intrigued by one patch quilts that use zillions of tiny pieces. It doesn't matter if a quilt is made from diamonds or hexagons or pyramids. My mind quickly goes from blown away by the beauty of these quilts to fascination of how did they do it?

I can't let it rest. I have fallen in love with geometric shapes and quilts with clean lines and a contemporary feel. I can't get enough, yet, I am daunted by the insane thought of needing templates and hand-piecing just because of an inset "Y" seam. Really, is that the only way? What I knew for sure is that I can't follow traditional rules. It's time to wipe the board clean and start anew. Fearless, I started by doing what I do best… I made a list.

- I need a method to accurately cut polygon shapes, template free. A perfect tool is one that also fits well in my hand.
- I don't want to remember what size strip is needed to cut a particular shape. I want to be able to cut strips in advance and decide later how to use them.
- I want the polygon shapes to play well with each other so I can combine them as my creativity expands.
- I want polygons small, but not micro-mini, and bold, but not chunky.
- And no hand stitching or marking sewing lines. I want to sew effortlessly.

Ask and you will receive. **The Polygon** and **Polygon2 Tools** have been formulated for perfect math…I've found the sweet spot. The tools play well together as Polymates, a marriage made in heaven. Each one cuts all four shapes to include the five-sided cone.

What gets you to effortless piecing of polygon shapes is the use of the **Butterfly Seam** technique to sew the inset pieces. It's an innovative approach to stitching that is harder to explain than it is to execute, yet it seals the love forever.

Polygon Affair is filled with ideas to make each quilt an original. I've designed a collection of blocks, connectors, and layout plans that are interchangeable to expand the possibilities. I want to entice you to journey with me through the stages of a love affair, a *Polygon Affair*… it's so easy you're bound to fall in love.

POLYGON AFFAIR 12 LOVE AT FIRST SIGHT

POLYGON AFFAIR 16 LOVE AT FIRST SIGHT

POLYGON AFFAIR 17 LOVE AT FIRST SIGHT

POLYGON AFFAIR 18 LOVE AT FIRST SIGHT

POLYGON AFFAIR 19 LOVE AT FIRST SIGHT

POLYGON AFFAIR | 25 | LOVE AT FIRST SIGHT

POLYGON AFFAIR 27 LOVE AT FIRST SIGHT

POLYGON AFFAIR   30   SEEING IS BELIEVING

HOW TO USE THE **POLYGON** AND **POLYGON 2** TOOL

diamonds.

Step 1. Cut a 3" strip for **Polygon Tool** or 5 ½" strip for **Polygon2 Tool.** Open strip to single layer and place the fabric right side up.

Step 2. Position the tool with the word "Polygon" pointing to the right. Cross cut into diamonds using the tool.

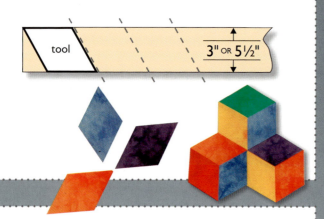

cones.

Step 1. Cut diamonds. (see diamonds)

Step 2. Place the **Polygon** or **Polygon2 Tool** with the cone mark even with the top edge of the cut diamond.

Step 3. Trim the top of the diamond on one end.

 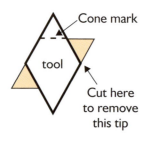 

hexagon.

Step 1. Cut diamond. (see diamonds)

Step 2. Place the **Polygon** or **Polygon2 Tool** with the hexagon mark even with the top edge of the cut diamond.

 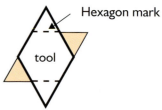

Step 3. Trim the tip of the diamond on both ends.

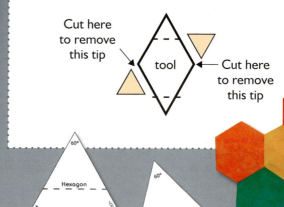

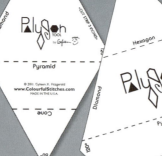 

POLYGON AFFAIR 32 SEEING IS BELIEVING

▲ pyramids.

Step 1. Cut a 3" strip for **Polygon Tool** or 5½" strip for **Polygon2 Tool**. Open strip to single layer and place the fabric right side up.

Step 2. Position the **Polygon** or **Polygon2 Tool** with the pyramid mark even with the bottom edge of the strip. Cut on both sides of the tool for the first pyramid. Note that the tip of the tool will be ¼" above the top edge of the strip.

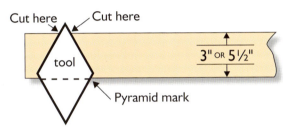

Step 3. Reverse the placement of the tool; align strip top edge with pyramid mark and side of the tool with the cut diagonal edge. Cut the second pyramid.

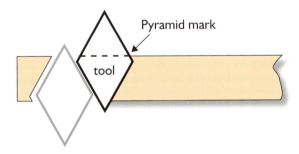

Step 4. Continue reversing and repeating of Step 3.

⬣ half hexagons.

Step 1. Cut a 3" strip. Open strip to single layer and place the fabric right side up.

Step 2. Position the **Polygon2 Tool** pyramid mark even with the bottom edge of the 3" strip and the hexagon mark even with the top edge of the 3" strip. Cut on both sides of the tool for the first half hexagon.

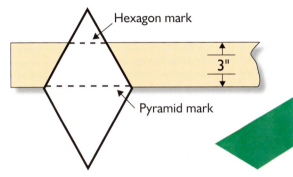

Step 3. Reverse the placement of the tool; align pyramid and hexagon marks between the top and bottom edges of the strip, and the side of the tool with the cut diagonal edge. Cut second half hexagon.

Step 4. Continue reversing tool and repeating step 3.

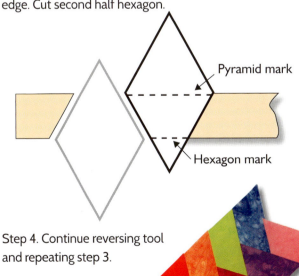

Butterfly Seam® TECHNIQUE

A **Butterfly Seam** can be used anytime THREE seams come together or for multiple seams that end at the same point. This method does not require marking or hand piecing. The beauty of it is in the creation of a Butterfly and the "unsewing." Let's begin:

Lay out the pieces to be stitched. **Figure 1**.

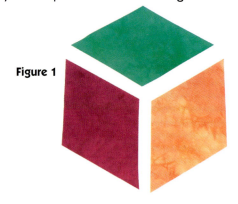

Figure 1

Sew seam ONE, **Figure 2**. Finger press to one side, **Figure 3**.

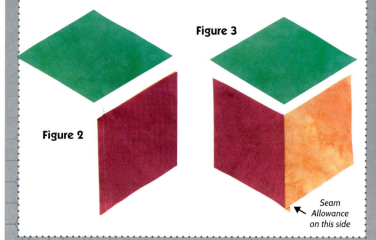

Figure 2

Figure 3

Seam Allowance on this side

Sew seam TWO (that is the side that DOES NOT have the seam allowance from seam one). Stitch across the entire side, **Figure 4**.

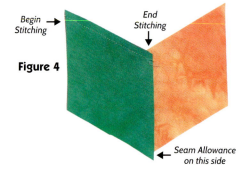

Begin Stitching

End Stitching

Figure 4

Seam Allowance on this side

Lay assembly right sides down on a table, **Figure 5**. Unsew all stitches that fall within the seam allowance, **Figure 6**. Try not to cut the thread just unsew or unstitch.

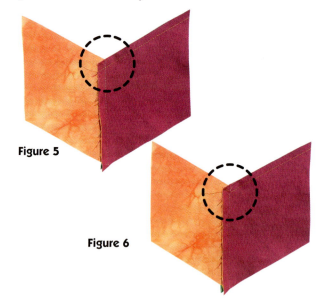

Figure 5

Figure 6

Seam THREE, is now a snap. From the wrong side, spread open seam 3, hence a Butterfly, **Figure 7**. You will notice that the two seams you just stitched will come together, **Figure 8**. You want to put them together such that the 1st seam is against the 2nd seam, the (4) cut edges are aligned AND they are wrong sides together. Pin to hold these seams (wings) together.

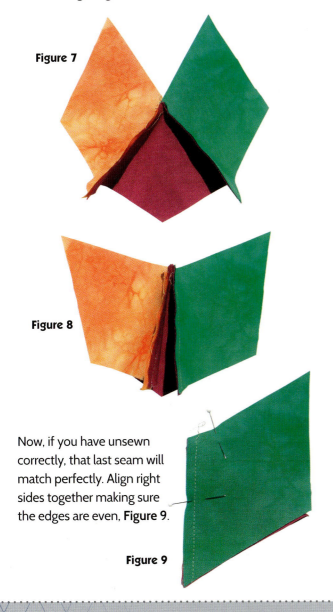

Figure 7

Figure 8

Now, if you have unsewn correctly, that last seam will match perfectly. Align right sides together making sure the edges are even, **Figure 9**.

Figure 9

Sew seam THREE. Stitch across the entire seam, **Figure 10**. Remove pins and unsew all stitches that fall within the seam allowance, **Figure 11**.

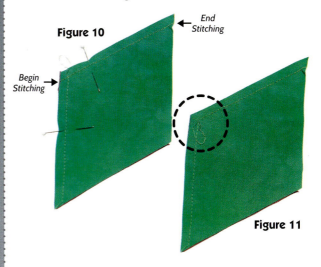

Figure 10 ← End Stitching

← Begin Stitching

Figure 11

Press the seams so they rotate and the center spins into a lovely hexagon, **Figure 12**. This will only work if ALL stitches have been removed in the seam allowance.

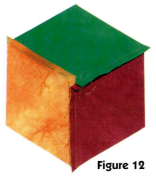

Figure 12

Done! **Figure 13**. I know it's unbelievable. It's that easy.

Figure 13

POLYGON AFFAIR   SEEING IS BELIEVING

Celebration
35" x 49"
Gyleen X. Fitzgerald
Quilted by Ashley Malinowski

PATTERN

Celebration

With ribbons spinning, the party has started. It's time to celebrate. No matter if it's a table runner or reconfigured for a lap quilt. Celebration is super quick to stitch. Who could ask for more?

Polygon Tool	Diamond
Polygon2 Tool	Pyramid
Block Size	10" x 11½"
Block Count	9

Supplies

(10) 3" x 40" strips, assorted fabric
½ yard for the setting pyramids
½ yard for binding

Instructions

1. Select (6) 3" x 40" strips, cut (2) diamonds using the Polygon Tool. Arrange diamonds per the sketch.

2. Stitch diamonds into pairs, this is seam 1. Repeat for the remainder of the diamonds. Make (6). Finger press seams to right.

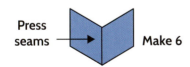

Press seams → Make 6

3. Stitch pairs together using a butterfly seam. Follow sketch numbers as a guide. Remember to move the seam allowance away from seam 2 if necessary before you begin to stitch. Make (3).

Note: The butterfly seam mantra is: seam one, seam two, unsew, wings together, pin, stitch last seam, unsew. Press.

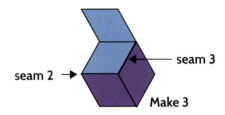

Make 3

4. Stitch the (3) segments together, again using a butterfly seam. Follow step 3 above to stitch segment 1 to segment 2. To stitch segment 3, follow stitching order on sketch 4a and 4b.

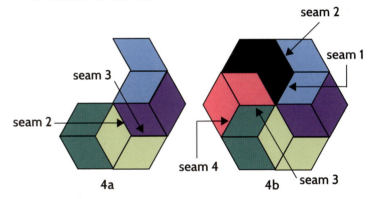

4a   4b

5. From the back of the block press center so that the seams rotate then press remaining seams from the front.

6. Repeat steps 1-5 to make (8) more Celebration blocks for a total of (9) blocks.

7. Using the setting pyramid fabric, cut (3) 5½" x 40" strips. Cross cut as many pyramids as possible with the Polygon2 Tool.

8. Place the Celebration blocks and pyramids in position as shown in sketch.

9. Stitch pyramids to ends of Celebration block then stitch block to block to form rows. Stitch rows to form the table runner.

10. Layer top with batting and backing. Quilt as you like.

11. Using the binding fabric, cut (4) 2½" x 40" strips. Sew strips end to end and fold lengthwise. Since the "corners" are 120 degrees and not the standard 90 degrees, you just need to be slightly more mindful of the corner turns. I stitched the binding with a ⅜" seam allowance to get a wider finished edge.

Seeing Stars

This Hexagon Star design has a wonderful graphic effect when it is combined with the Polygon2 pyramid. I can see this expanded to a lap or bed quilt by making more stars from scrap 3" strips. **Seeing Stars** is an old school pattern updated to be modern using contemporary colors and the Butterfly Seam.

Nightfall and Sunrise
50" x 38"
Gyleen X. Fitzgerald
Quilted by Beth Hanlon-Ridder

PATTERN

Nightfall and Sunrise

The sky looks surreal as I watch those flaming reds and cadet blues vanish in the night, only to see them again with the rising sun. Using batik fabrics gives this wall-hanging a watercolor feeling like a Monet painting. Oh, I'm not exactly comparing my design directly to his. I'm just thinking, what a nice, easy way to create great art! Picture this in shades of lavender and green for wisteria and foliage. Or, if you get really inspired, why not try an abstract landscape.

Polygon Tool	Cone

Supplies

20 strips 3" x 22" for color group A
20 strips 3" x 22" for color group B
¼ yard from color group A (border 1)
¼ yard from color group B (border 2)
½ yard for border 3
2 yards for backing and binding

Instructions

1. Using the Polygon Tool and 3" x 22" strips, align fabric edge with edge of the tool. Cut (5 to 6) diamonds across the 22" width of fabric from each strip.

2. Place the Polygon Tool cone mark even with the top edge of the cut diamond, outside edges will align. Trim the tip of the diamond on one end.

Note: Color group A forms the dominate 4 bars
Color group B forms the background and edge of bars
1 cone color group A + 1 cone color group B = 1 set
12 sets = 1 column
8 columns (4 right + 4 left) = 1 quilt

3. Cone to cone assembly–right: Randomly pair up (1) cone from color group A with (1) cone from color group B for 12 pairs. Sew into sets by placing the A cone on top of the B cone, right-sides together. Sew along the right long edge of cone A. See sketch. Press seam to one side.

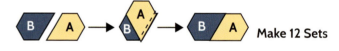 Make 12 Sets

4. Column assembly–right: Position the cone assembly in a line with long edges touching.

Note: all diagonal seams slant in the same direction. Sew (12) cone assemblies together along the long edge making a column with color group A on the right, press seams down.

5. Repeat Step 3 and 4 to make (4 right) columns.

6. Cone to cone assembly–left: Randomly pair up (1) cone from color group A with (1) cone from color group B for 12 pairs. Sew into sets by placing the B cone on top of A cone, right-sides together. Sew along the right long edge of cone B. See sketch. Press seam to one side.

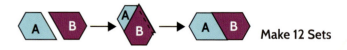 Make 12 Sets

7. Column assembly–left: Position the cone assembly in a line with long edges touching. You should notice that all the diagonal seams are slanting in the same direction. Sew (12) cone assemblies together on the long edge to make a column. Position column so that color group B is on the left, press seams down.

8. Repeat Step 6 and 7 to make (4 left) columns.

9. Lay the columns alternating between right and left columns. The quilt starts with a right column and ends with a right column. Number the columns in the order of your placement. Position the left columns half a cone assembly down from the right columns. They fit together in a zig-zag pattern. See stetch.

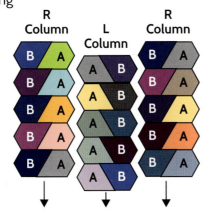

10. Stitch columns together using a butterfly seam: Start at the top of the column making sure all seams are pointing down. Seam 1 is already completed; you are stitching seams 2 and 3. Repeat until columns 3-8 are joined. Press seams from the front. Yes, this is messy on the back but looks perfect from the front.

11. Square up quilt top: Trim top of quilt even with columns 2, 4, 6 and 8. Trim the bottom of quilt even with columns 1, 3, 5 and 7. Trim the sides even with lowest zig-zag point.

12. For border 1, cut (4) strips 1½" x 40" from color group B. Sew strips end to end. Measure quilt from top to bottom; cross cut (2) strips to this length and stitch to sides of the quilt. Press seams toward border.

13. Measure quilt from side to side; cross cut (2) strips to this length and stitch to the top and bottom of quilt. Press seams toward border.

14. For border 2 and border 3, repeat Steps 12 and 13 using (4) 1" x 40" strips from color group A (border 2) and (5) 4" x 40" strips from border fabric (border 3).

15. Layer backing, batting and quilt top. Baste layers together, quilt as you like.

16. Make binding by connecting (5) 2½" x 40" strips end to end. Fold and press in half lengthwise for a double binding. Match raw edges of binding to raw edge of quilt top. Stitch in place. Turn folded edge to back of quilt and stitch in place.

17. Make a label to identify this quilt as being your art; add a hanging sleeve and enjoy.

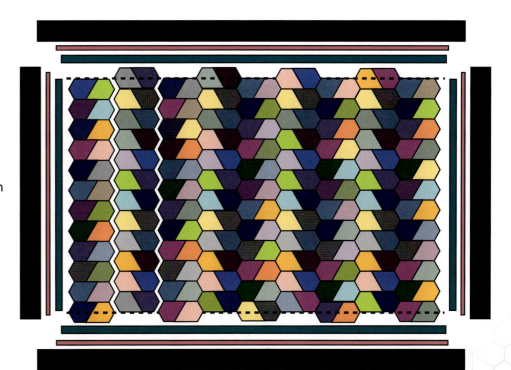

POLYGON AFFAIR • SINGLE & LOVING IT

Beth's design was inspired by **Garden in the Mist** *(see inset)*. What I love about Beth's design is it shows just how striking a substitution can be. Beth omitted the Polygon2 pyramids and replaced them with Polygon2 diamonds. The end result is clean and crisp… on the edge of modern.

Diamonds are a Girl's BFF
32" x 39"
Beth Hanlon-Ridder

Promise Me Diamonds
30" x 37"
Dorothy Reel

Diamonds… A Girl's BFF
79" x 90"
Patti Castoe

Garden in the Mist
Diamonds Are a Girl's Best Friend.

Why? Because they sparkle and are fun! Go with me on this. The style or mood is created by your choice of border and rest of the fabrics are supporting cast. The super light and super dark fabrics used for the pyramids sets the diamonds. I love the fresh modern look of a "stripy" quilt; they can be as long or short as you need with rows added or deleted as desired.

Courtship of Seven Sisters
91" x 93"
Gyleen X. Fitzgerald
Quilted by Ashley Malinowski

PATTERN

Courtship of Seven Sisters

Nothing is more stunning than brilliant stars made from diamonds. The Seven Sisters block makes this quilt sparkle. I surrounded the stars with diamond bowtie connectors to make the quilt dance. The sample is a charm quilt meaning each diamond is a different fabric. They are fun to collect and exchange with friends.

Polygon Tool	Diamond & Pyramid
Polygon2 Tool	Diamond & Pyramid
Block Size	23" x 20"
Block Count	25

Supplies

(31) 5½" x 40" strips for Polygon2 diamonds and pyramids
²/₃ yard white for connector diamonds and pyramids
½ yard black for connector pyramids
2 yards for border
1 yard for binding

Note: For a charm quilt, cut (154) Polygon2 diamonds and cut (32) Polygon2 pyramids from different fabrics.

Instructions

1. Using the Polygon2 Tool, cut (5) diamonds from each of the 31 strips. Be sure to open the strip to a single layer. Cut (154) total.

2. Using the remainder of the strips, cut as many Polygon2 pyramids as possible. Cut (32) total.

3. Using white connector fabric, cut several 3" strips. Cross cut using the Polygon Tool into diamonds and pyramids. Cut more as needed.

4. Using the black connector fabric, cut several 3" strips. Cross cut using the Polygon Tool into pyramids. Cut more as needed.

5. For a connector assembly, use (2) white diamonds, (2) white pyramids and (2) black pyramids. To assemble, sew the white and black pyramids together to form a diamond assembly. Make (2). Sew the diamond assembly to a white diamond. Make (2). Then sew the assembly together, press seam open. Make (3) diamond "bowtie" connector assemblies to get started, make more as needed. See sketch.

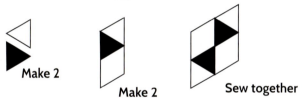

Make 2   Make 2   Sew together

6. Using (2) Polygon2 diamonds and (1) diamond bowtie connector, lay pieces per the sketch to form a tumbling block.

7. Following sketch, sew diamond to diamond. Finger press seam to the right. Use straight pins at the beginning and end to keep the seams together and to reduce stretching.

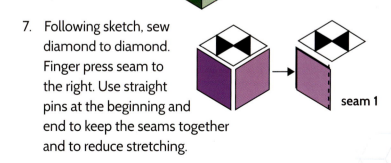

seam 1

8. Lay the diamond bowtie connector directly on top of the left diamond. Check the alignment of the points. Again, pin the beginning and end to keep seams together and to reduce stretching. Sew the seam. Unsew all stitching in the seam allowance. Try not to cut the thread, just unstitch.

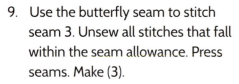
Back of bowtie connector

9. Use the butterfly seam to stitch seam 3. Unsew all stitches that fall within the seam allowance. Press seams. Make (3).

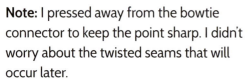

Note: I pressed away from the bowtie connector to keep the point sharp. I didn't worry about the twisted seams that will occur later.

10. Position the (3) blocks so that the bowtie connector is to the outside. See sketch.

11. Join the (3) blocks with a butterfly seam. At this point, you will repeat the stitching order and ignore the sub-piecing. Pretend that you are just stitching diamonds. Flip the seam allowance if it needs to be on the other side.

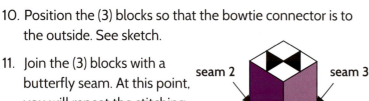

12. For seam 3, you should have (4) notches (dog-ears) AND all sub-piecing seams on top of each other. Pin to hold the wings together and pin beginning and end of seam; and sew. Repeat to make (23) stars.

13. Begin to layout the stars in columns; they will nest together. Sew star to star using butterfly seams. Make (3) columns with 5 stars and (2) columns with 4 stars.

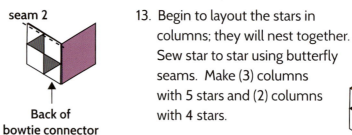

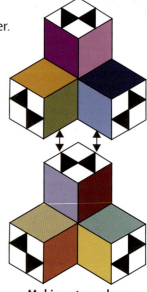
Making star column

14. Add partial stars to top and bottom of the columns with 4 stars.

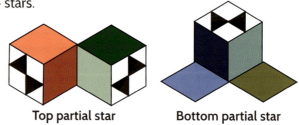
Top partial star   Bottom partial star

15. To make the body of the quilt top, join the columns together using butterfly seams. Begin with 5 star column and alternate with the 4 star column. The columns will nest together.

16. Using the border fabric, cut several 5½" strips. Cross cut (16) Polygon2 diamonds and (46) Polygon2 pyramids.

17. Make (5) right side and (5) left side edge fillers using Polygon2 pyramids and bowtie connectors. See sketch.

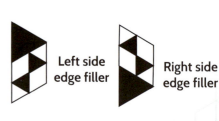
Left side edge filler   Right side edge filler

POLYGON AFFAIR   48   FIRST DATE

19. Using a butterfly seam, insert the edge filler assemblies to both sides of the quilt.

20. Insert the Polygon2 border diamonds across the top and bottom of quilt. Trim excess to a straight edge.

21. Sew Polygon2 (17) border pyramids and (16) star fabric pyramids together, alternating. Make (2). Stitch to sides of quilt and trim even with the edge.

22. Layer backing, batting, and quilt top. Quilt as desired. The sample was quilted edge-to-edge on a longarm machine, however for a more modern look, try doing a utility stitch with #8 perle cotton.

23. To make binding, cut (10) 2½" x 40" strips and connect end to end. Press strip in half lengthwise for a double binding. Sew binding to quilt.

24. Make a label to identify this quilt as being your art.

Atlantis

If a bed quilt is not your thing, try switching to the Polygon Tool and 3" strips to make a wall-hanging. Atlantis is a variation on the classic Seven Sisters and with black diamonds has a contemporary look. I never thought unsewing would be my friend, however, using it for a butterfly seam is the key to quick accurate piecing.

Star Struck
21" x 80"
Gyleen X. Fitzgerald
Quilted by Ashley Malinowski

PATTERN

Star Struck

I'm mesmerized by the thought that four star blocks can span 80". Wow! I'm in love and I just want to sing out loud. Star Struck is designed to incorporate a variety of fabrics and use what you have on hand. It's my new way of thinking. If your first date with Star Struck goes too fast just keep going and make a bed quilt.

Polygon Tool	Diamond & Pyramid
Polygon2 Tool	Diamond & Pyramid
Block Size	23" x 20"
Block Count	4

Supplies

When selecting your fabrics, refer to the block diagram to the right.

Soloist (S): This is the feature fabric and, like a soloist, will make your quilt sing. Too many variations will cause disruption. Be wise and select only one. A fat quarter (22" x 18") is all you'll need.

Harmonizer (H): This is the voice that blends with or goes between the soloist and the choir. Choose the voice that has range. A fat quarter (22" x 18") will work.

Choir (1, 2, 3): This is where you have the variety. These are the voices that are nice and steady, but don't have the pizzazz to make it as a soloist. You will need (12) 3" x 40" strips.

Background (B): This provides the stage; a platform on which to perform. One yard is perfect or use several pieces that read the same in value.

Instructions

The mantra for Star Struck is six; you will cut just about (6) of everything.

1. To cut for (1) star: select (3) fabrics from the choir, cross cut (6) Polygon diamonds from each fabric; using the harmonizer fabric, cut several 3" x 22" strips then cross cut (6) Polygon pyramids; using the soloist, cut a 5½" x 22" strip then cross cut (1) Polygon2 hexagon; and using the background, cut (1) 5½" x 40" strip then cross cut (6) Polygon2 diamonds.

2. Layout the star per the sketch. The numbers in the diamonds respond to choir fabric 1, 2 or 3, "H" is harmonizer, "S" is soloist and "B" is background.

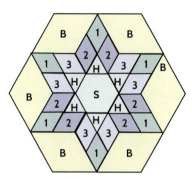

3. Stitch the points. You can do some speed stitching here by making (3) at a time since they are identical. Sew the points like a 4-patch. Don't trim any dog ears; they are the alignment points. Pressed last seam open to get a flat center. Make (3) points then repeat step 3, for the remaining (3) points. You now have (2) groups of points.

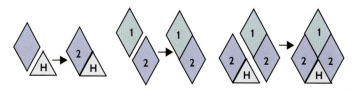

4. Sew the points to the Polygon2 hexagon. The easiest way to do this is to sew points to each other to form a ring (all but the last seam to close the ring).

5. Then sew the hexagon center to the ring using the butterfly seam. Finger press instead of ironing so the seams will be flexible to flip if necessary. The last seam is to close the ring.

6. Using a butterfly seam, insert the Polygon2 background diamond between the points. Note that seam 1 is the seam connecting the star points. Press seams toward the Polygon2 diamonds. The last seam is to close the ring.

7. Repeat steps 1-6 (3) more times to make a total of (4) Star Struck blocks.

8. Stitch Star Struck blocks together to form a column.

9. You will need (6) connectors which will fill the big "V" between Star Struck blocks. Using the soloist, cut a 3" x 22" strip then cross cut (6) Polygon diamonds. Using the harmonizer fabric, cut several 3" x 22" strips then cross cut (12) Polygon2 half hexagons. To cut a half hexagon, align the 3" strip between the "pyramid" and "hexagon" marking on the Polygon2 Tool.

10. Layout connector per sketch using (1) diamond and (2) half hexagons. Sew together using a butterfly seam. Press with rotating seams. Make (6) connectors.

11. Stitch one connector into the big "V" of the Star Struck column runner using a butterfly seam.

12. Layer backing, batting, and quilt top. Quilt as desired.

13. Using the binding fabric cut 2" bias strips, connecting them end to end until the length is 12" longer than the distance around the table runner. Fold and press in half lengthwise for a double binding. Sew binding to quilt.

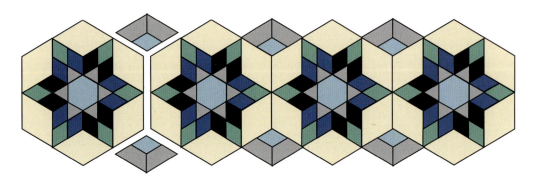

Bed Runner or Bed Quilt Connectors

The gallery of quilts expands the possibility of the Star Struck design. You can add connectors for a bed quilt or edge pieces if you prefer a straight edge finish.

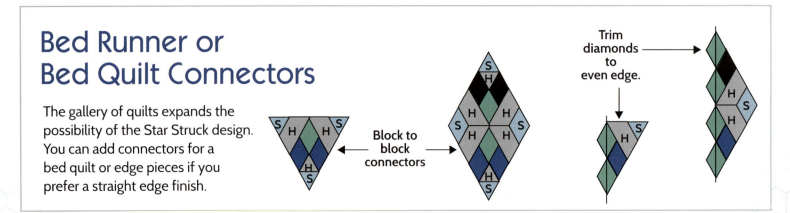

Block to block connectors

Trim diamonds to even edge.

Christmas Choir
24" x 60"
Virginia Hodge

Stars Over the Savanna
48" x 54"
Gail E. Copper Milburn

Autumn Blossoms
78" x 84"
Pamela S. Barrows

Peaceful Stars
30" x 90"
Nancy St. Pierre

POLYGON AFFAIR   FIRST DATE

Star Struck Doggies
47" x 42"
Jane Adler

Sayomi Stars
19" x 79"
Pat Dews

Stars and Stripes
83" x 94"
Judy Wilson

Nara Garden Stars
76" x 81"
Kathy McLaren

Matchmaker
67" x 60"
Gyleen X. Fitzgerald
Quilted by Maria O'Haver

PATTERN

Matchmaker

Find me a match. I love playing concentration where the cards are turned over and you pick two at a time until you get a pair. It's fun, but exhausting. Are you doing the same looking for your perfect match in a soulmate? Enter the matchmaker. This quilt was designed in honor of Melanie who knew my perfect match. It is bold, fun, and easy to stitch.

Polygon Tool	Diamond
Polygon2 Tool	Cones & Pyramid

Supplies

(14) 5½" x 40" strips, assorted fabrics for Polygon2 cones
½ yard for Polygon diamonds
½ yard for Polygon2 pyramids
⅓ yard for edge wedges
¾ yard for sashing
1 yard for border
¾ yard binding

Instructions

1. Using the Polygon2 Tool and 5½" x 40" strips, align fabric edge with edge of the tool. Cut (4) diamonds from each strip; use a single layer of each strip.

2. Cross cut into the cone shape and group them into 2 pairs.

3. Using the diamond fabric, cut (4) 3" x 40" strips. Cross cut (30) Polygon diamonds.

4. Using the Polygon2 pyramid fabric, cut (3) 5½" x 40" strips. Cross cut (48) Polygon2 pyramids.

5. Join the cones by stitching across the top side. Finger press seam to the side. Make (27) pairs.

6. Insert the Polygon diamonds on the left side of the cone pairs using a butterfly seam. Make (27).

7. Sew Polygon2 pyramids to the top and bottom of the right side of the cone assembly. Make (24). See sketch.

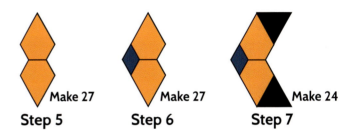

8. Layout 3 rows of cone assemblies. Sew (8) cones assemblies together omitting the 9th assembly to form the rows.

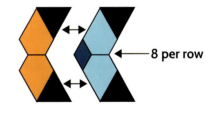

9. Using the edge wedge fabric, cut (6) 9¼" x 5¼" rectangles. Layer (2) right sides together and cut across on the diagonal. See sketch below. Repeat for the remaining rectangles.

10. Sew edge wedges to the left end of each row. Square off if necessary for a straight edge.

11. Using the remaining (3) cones assemblies, insert a Polygon diamond to the right side of assembly then add edge wedges to the right side.

Left Side Step 10   Right Side Step 11

12. Sew the last completed cone assembly to the right side each row. Square off if necessary for a straight edge.

13. Using the sashing fabric, cut (9) 2½" x 40" strips. Sew strips end to end.

14. Measure the length of cone rows. Cross cut (4) strips of sashing to this length. Sew sashing between the rows to join them and at top and bottom. Press seams toward sashing.

15. Measure quilt from top to bottom. Cross cut (2) strips to this length. Sew to sides of quilt. Press seams toward sashing.

16. Using the border fabric, cut (9) 4½" x 40" strips. Sew strips end to end.

17. Measure quilt from top to bottom; cross cut (2) strips to this length and stitch to sides of the quilt. Press seams toward border.

18. Measure quilt from side to side; cross cut (2) strips to this length and stitch to the top and bottom of quilt. Press seams toward border.

19. Layer backing, batting and quilt top. Baste layers together, quilt as you like.

20. Using the binding fabric, cut (9) 2½" x 40" strips. Sew end to end, fold and press in half lengthwise for a double binding. Match raw edges of binding to raw edge of quilt top. Stitch in place. Turn folded edge to back of quilt and stitch in place.

Garden of Eden
71" x 70"
Gyleen X. Fitzgerald
Quilted by Maria O'Haver

PATTERN

Garden of Eden

Bold flowers, like seductive Begonias, combined with a simple connector form the labyrinth in the Garden of Eden. Don't let the complex appearance fool you; it's a contemporary variation of Grandmother's Flower Garden.

Polygon Tool	Diamond & Pyramid
Polygon2 Tool	Hexagon
Block Size	15" x 17"
Block Count	14

Supplies

(16) 5½" x 40" strips for flowers
½ yard for flower centers
1 yard for leaves
½ yard path (diamonds)
½ yard garden (pyramids)
¾ yard for edge (diamonds) and border 1
1 yard for border 2
⅔ yard for binding

Instructions

1. Using (12) flower strips and Polygon2 Tool, open strip to one layer and cut (6) Polygon2 diamonds then cross cut into Polygon2 hexagons.

2. Using flower center fabric, cut (3) 5½" x 40" strips. Open strips to one layer and cut (12) Polygon2 diamonds. Cross cut (12) Polygon2 hexagons.

3. Lay out the flower using (6) flowers hexagons and (1) center hexagon; sew a "ring" of flower hexagons first (all but the last seam to close the ring). Then start doing the butterfly seam to insert the center hexagon. The last seam is to close the ring.

4. Make (12) begonia flowers.

5. Using the leaf fabric, cut (8) 3" x 40" strips. Using the Polygon Tool, cross cut (84) Polygon diamonds. Each flower will need (6) leaves.

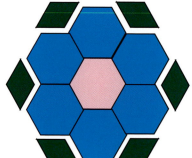

6. Insert each leaf using butterfly seams. Note that seam 1 is already complete and is part of the flower.

7. The connectors are next. I think of these as the pathway through the garden. Cut both the diamond and pyramid fabrics into 3" x 40" strips. Using the Polygon Tool, cross cut (72) Polygon pyramids and (72) Polygon diamonds.

8. Layout connector assembly per sketch. Sew diamond to pyramid. Make (74). Then sew (3) together using a butterfly seam. Make (24) connectors.

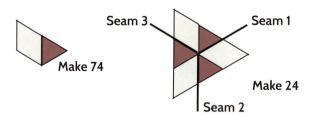

9. Layout flowers per sketch with 3 full flowers on each row.

10. Sew connector assembly to opposite sides of flower to form a diamond shape. See sketch.

11. Sew (3) flower assemblies together to form rows. Make (4) rows. See sketch.

12. To complete the edge follow the sketch to make (2) half flowers; (2) partial flowers; and (2) smidgens for the corner.

13. Half and partial flowers: Using the remaining (4) flower strips cut the following from each strip: cut (2) Polygon2 diamonds and cross cut into (2) Polygon2 hexagons. Trim the remaining strip to 3" wide. Then, using the Polygon Tool, cut (2) polygon diamonds.

14. Using the center fabric, trim the remaining to 3". Cross cut (4) polygon diamonds using the Polygon Tool.

15. Sew together using a butterfly seam following the placement and sew in the order shown in the sketch. Make (4). See sketch (Unit A).

16. Cut the edge fabric into (3) 3" x 40" strips. Cross cut (26) polygon diamonds using the Polygon Tool.

17. Sew an edge diamond to both sides of the flower polygon diamonds. Make (8). See sketch (Unit B).

18. Sew edge assemblies to either side of the hexagon flower assembly. Make (4). See sketch.

19. Sew leaf polygon diamond to connector diamond to a connector pyramid then to an edge diamond. Make (2) right then make (4) left mirror image. See sketch (Unit C).

20. Insert assembly from step 19 on both sides of the half flower assembly completing the butterfly seam. Make (2). See sketch.

21. Add the half flower assembly to end of 2nd and 3rd rows.

22. For partial flowers, insert Unit C to left side of Unit A and add leaf diamond to the right side. Make (2). See sketch.

23. Add partial flowers to the end of 1st and 4th rows.

24. To complete the edge of the quilt top, make (2) smidgen assemblies by adding edge diamonds to step 8 assembly. See sketch.

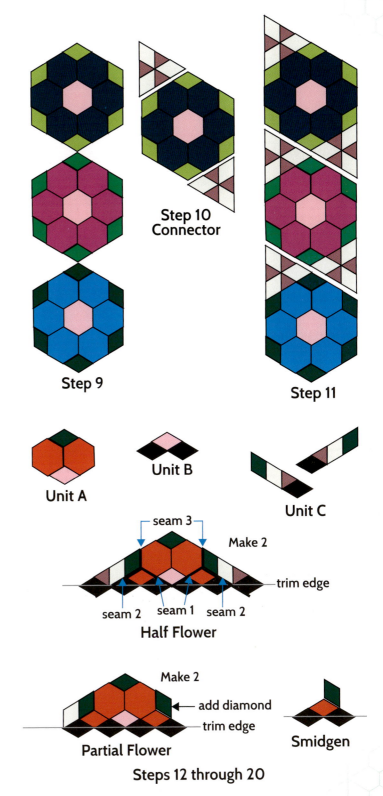

POLYGON AFFAIR   MEET AND GREET FRIENDS

25. Add to the smidgen to rows 1 and 4 to complete the quilt top. Trim all edge diamonds for a straight edge.

26. Using border 1 fabric cut (2) 1½" x 40" and cut (2) 3½" x 40" strips. Sew corresponding strips end to end.

27. Measure quilt from side to side, cross cut (2) of the 1½" border strip to this measurement and add to the top and bottom of the quilt. Press seam to the border.

28. Measure quilt from top to bottom, cross cut (2) of the 3½" border strips to this measurement and add to the both sides of the quilt. Press seam towards the border.

29. Using border 2 fabric, cut (7) 3½" x 40" strips. Sew end to end.

30. Measure quilt from side to side, cross cut (2) strips to this measurement and add to the top and bottom of the quilt. Press seam towards the border.

31. Measure quilt from top to bottom, cross cut (2) strips to this measurement and add to the both sides of the quilt. Press seam towards the border.

32. Layer backing, batting and quilt top. Quilt as desired. The sample was quilted edge to edge on a longarm machine.

33. Using binding fabric, cut (7) 2½" x 40" strips and sew end to end. Press strip in half lengthwise for a double binding. Sew binding to quilt.

Grandmother's Flower Garden

Grandmother's Flower Garden is a classic with or without a pathway. Lois's quilt is a remake of my antique quilt and uses the Polygon Tool to make a smaller flower. The addition of hexagon leaves in the traditional pathway sets the garden in rows. Yet, the same flowers would have a contemporary appeal if sewn flower to flower without a pathway. Take it one step further for a modern look by using Polygon2 for bold flowers. Substitute any of the Flower Girl designs (see page 120) for endless possibilities. In either size, the garden is always beautiful when bursting with flowers.

Grandmother's Flower Garden Revisited
57" x 70"
Lois W. Bruno

Petals and Wings
62" x 62"
Caroline Frey Mounvier-Vehier

Summer Breeze
68" x 68"
Lynn Van Keuren

Dean's Fuji Garden
67" x 68"
Carol Hansen

Garden of Eden
66" x 67"
Pat Dews

Who is in My Garden?
72" x 75"
Bonnie Doher Gustafson

POLYGON AFFAIR 63 MEET AND GREET FRIENDS

Garden Delight
68" x 68"
Virginia Hodge

Hawaiian Honeymoon
65" x 65"
Shirley Rose Winn

Garden of Eden–Batik
68" x 68"
Deborah R. Brobst

Garden of Eden
67" x 67"
Rellajeanne W. Cook

Garden of Eden
64" x 66"
Vicki M. McCormick

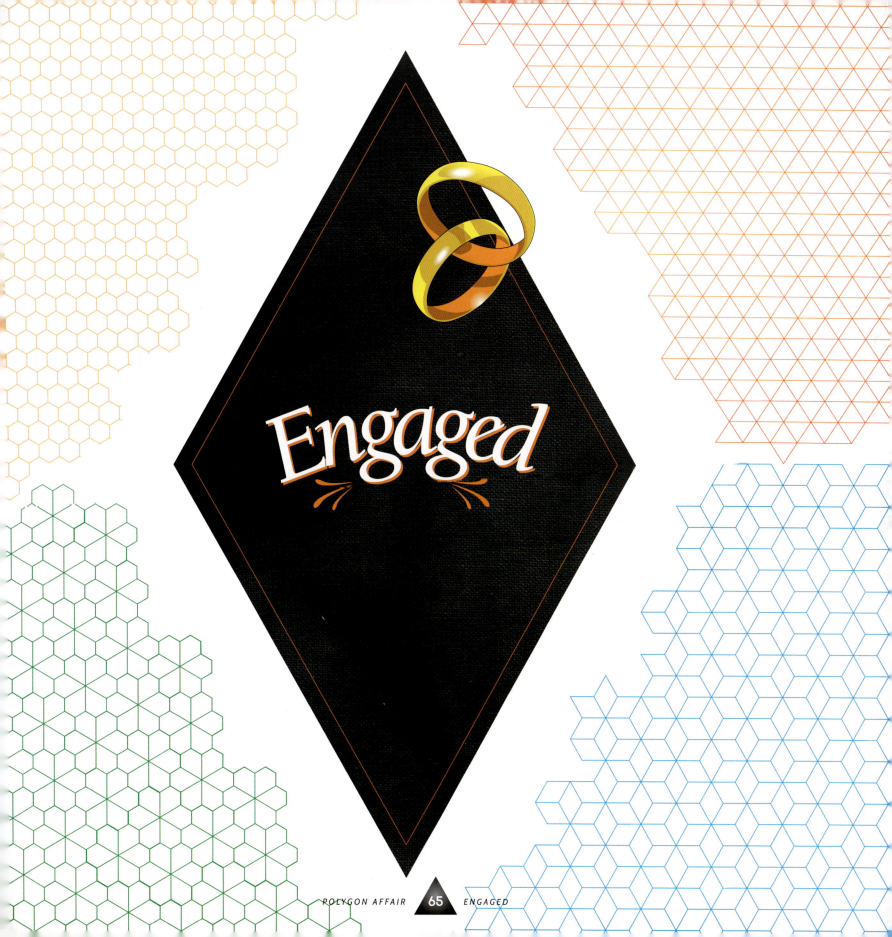

Engaged
72" x 73"
Gyleen X. Fitzgerald
Quilted by Beth Hanlon-Ridder

PATTERN

Engaged

The excitement of a pending marriage…oh, what a feeling. Stars twinkle in the sky and sparkle in your loved one's eyes. Engaged dazzles by using all four polygon shapes. The design looks equally spectacular if made using Polygon2 Tool. Just remember to adjust the fabric requirements and use 5½" strips.

Polygon Tool	Diamond, Cone, Hexagon & Pyramid
Block Size	11½" x 10"
Block Count	32

Supplies

64 strips 3" x 40" in assortment of fabric for hexagon stars
1½ yard for focus pyramid and edge fabric
2 yards for background pyramids and border 1
½ yard for border 2
1 yard for border 3
⅔ yard for backing and binding

Instructions

1. Using the Polygon Tool and 3" x 40" strips, aligned fabric edge with edge of the tool. Cut (13) diamonds from each strip; use a single layer of each strip.

2. Cross cut (6) of the diamonds into the cone shape and cross cut (1) diamond into the hexagon shape.

3. For each pieced hexagon star, you will need (6) diamonds, (6) cones and (1) hexagon. Build (32) sets mixing and matching so the diamond, cone, and hexagon are different print fabrics for each block. It's okay for some hexagon stars to have high contrast while others have low contrast.

4. Layout (1) hexagon star per the sketch before you begin stitching. For the hexagon star stitching order of assembly, follow sketch.

Note: It really doesn't matter where you begin to stitch and I don't think one way is more efficient than another. The key to avoid confusion is to lay out the full block next to your machine so you know what goes where. In the sketch, I've numbered the order of sewing the seams; remember to move the seam allowance if necessary to stitch seam 2 of the butterfly seam.

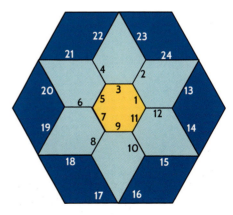

5. Cut at least (3) 3" x 40" strips from the focus pyramid and background pyramid fabrics. Cross cut as many pyramids as possible across the full width using the Polygon Tool. (Cut more strips and pyramids as needed to complete the quilt.)

6. Lay out pyramid connector assembly with background pyramids on the tips #1, #3 and #4 and focus pyramid in the center #2.

POLYGON AFFAIR · 67 · ENGAGED

7. Sew pyramid 1, 3 and 4 to center 2. Finger PRESS (do not iron) toward background pyramid after each seam. To keep pyramids in alignment, use pins especially to hold the beginning and end of the seam. Note: with pyramids, the "corner ears" help alignment. Position the "missing ear" corner against a pointed ear corner. Don't trim the "ears" off. Make (32) pyramid connectors.

8. Sew (2) pyramid connector assemblies to opposite sides of hexagon stars. Press seams toward pyramid connector assembly.

9. Using the (32) pieced hexagon assemblies, position them (5) across and (4) across in alternating rows. They will be staggered and nested. Sew block to block to form rows. Rows with (5) hexagon assemblies do not have pyramid connector assemblies on the ends. Rows with (4) hexagon assemblies have (2) pyramid connector assemblies. Add or remove pyramid connectors as needed.

10. Sew row to row; matching seams.

11. Using 3" strips of background pyramid fabric, cut (24) diamonds with the Polygon Tool. Layout a diamond connector assembly. Sew focus fabric pyramid to background fabric pyramid to form a diamond, make 2. Sew diamond assembly to background diamonds. Make 2, then sew together. Make 6 diamond connector assemblies.

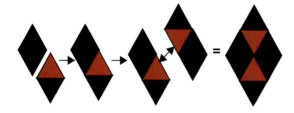

12. At this point, the rows are jagged and need setting triangles. Using focus pyramid fabric cut several strips 32" x 40". Open strip to full length; to cut the triangles align the 30° line from your 24" rotary cutter ruler even with the top of the strip for the FIRST CUT. When making the second cut, align the cut 1st cut edge to the 60° line for each triangle. Cut (14) triangles total. See sketch.

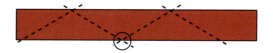

13. Sew large triangle to both sides of the diamond connector forming a flat HUGE triangle per sketch. Press seams toward the large triangles. Make (6).

14. Unstitch about 1" of the row with 4 Hexagon Stars; sew the HUGE triangle assembly to this edge. Seam A in sketch below. Press seams.

15. Complete the seam for the open side of the HUGE triangle. Seam B in sketch below. You should be able to align all seams.

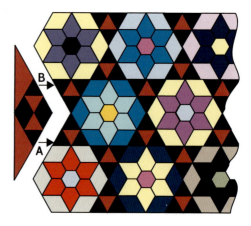

16. Divide (2) large triangles (cut in step 12) in half and sew to corners.

17. At this point, the edge of the quilt top should be straight. You may need to trim; just be mindful to leave ¼" for seam allowance.

18. For border 1, cut (8) 1¾" x 40" strips. Sew strips end to end. Measure quilt from side to side; cross cut (2) strips to this length and stitch to the top and bottom of quilt. Press seams toward border.

19. Measure quilt from top to bottom; cross cut (2) strips to this length and stitch to sides of the quilt. Press seams toward border.

20. For border 2, cut (4) 2¼" x 40" strips. Sew strips end to end. Measure quilt from top to bottom; cross cut (2) strips to this length and stitch to sides of the quilt. Press seams toward border.

21. For border 3, cut (4) 5" x 40" strips. Sew strips end to end. Measure quilt from top to bottom; cross cut (2) strips to this length and stitch to sides of the quilt. Press seams toward border.

22. Layer backing, batting and quilt top. Baste layers together, quilt as you like.

23. Make binding by connecting (8) 2½" x 40" strips. Fold and press in half lengthwise for a double binding. Stitch in place.

POLYGON AFFAIR ENGAGED

Polygon Affair in Houston
78" x 94"
Lorraine Carter

1930's Engaged
56" x 64"
Deborah R. Brobst

Why is it that, if you wait long enough, what is considered antique or old is reinvented and a called contemporary? Pieced hexagon blocks have been with us since the 1920s. Proof is what Peg Bingham discovered when researching *Wanda Drachenberg-Klann's circa 1940/1950*s quilt. Peg describes Wanda's unfinished Hexagon Star top and states, "They are constructed with a combination of machine piecing and appliqué stitches; the star pieces and the insetting diamonds are machine stitched while the hexagons are applied on top of the stars with appliqué stitches." Amazing...so would Wanda have finished her Hexagon Star if she had known how to do a Butterfly Seam?

I met Valerie Herrmann a few years ago in Tennessee while teaching my Engaged workshop. She told me about a Hexagon Star quilt she received from her husband's friend who moved to this country from Japan. The friend was given a Hexagon Star quilt from the family he stayed with in Texas upon arrival in America. He had very few personal possessions and used the quilt to keep warm in the winter. The friend, knowing she was a quilter, one day showed her his quilt. To Valerie's surprise, when he moved to a different town, he gave her the quilt. Valerie was kind enough to bring it to class and WOW! I could not take my eyes off all the beautiful stars and just loved the idea of their shared inset diamonds. Peg's research identified this as The Star and Box Quilt pattern, originally printed in 1939. Love exists in many forms and quilts are tied to our hearts. Engaged, reinvented for today.

Butterflies
40" x 47"
Gyleen X. Fitzgerald
Quilted by Beth Hanlon-Ridder

PATTERN

Butterflies

So, how do you know it's love? Are you giddy? And your nerves of steel are broken? Excited, you're floating like a butterfly? Then for sure its love.

Polygon Tool	Diamond & Pyramid
Polygon2 Tool	Diamond
Block Size	10" x 11½"
Block Count	20

Supplies

1 yard medium fabric, solid or semi-solid
1 yard dark fabric, solid or semi-solid
1 yard light fabric, solid or semi-solid
(10) 3" x 22" assorted accent fabric (batik, solid or semi-solid)
½ yard for binding

Instructions

1. Cut (3) 5½" x 40" strips from light, medium and dark fabric. From the light fabric strips, cross cut using the Polygon2 Tool (15) Polygon2 diamonds and (6) Polygon2 pyramids. From the medium fabric strips, cross cut using the Polygon2 Tool (16) Polygon2 diamonds and (4) Polygon2 pyramids. From the dark fabric, cross cut (10) Polygon2 diamonds and (4) Polygon2 pyramids.

2. Cut (2) 3" x 40" strips from light fabric, cross cut using the Polygon Tool (12) Polygon diamonds and (12) Polygon pyramids.

3. Cut (1) 3" x 40" strips from medium fabric, cross cut using the Polygon Tool (8) Polygon diamonds and (8) Polygon pyramids.

4. Cut (3) 3" x 40" strips from dark fabric, cross cut using the Polygon Tool (20) Polygon diamonds and (20) Polygon pyramids.

5. Using the (10) 3" x 22" strips, cut (40) Polygon pyramids using the Polygon Tool.

6. For a diamond connector, use (2) light Polygon diamonds, (2) light Polygon pyramids and (2) accent Polygon pyramids. To assemble, sew the light and accent pyramids together to form a diamond assembly. Make (2). Sew the diamond assembly to a light diamond. Make (2). Then sew the assembly together, press seam open. Make (6) light diamond "butterfly" connector assemblies. Repeat with medium and dark fabric. Make (4) medium and (10) dark diamond "butterflies". See sketch.

   Make 6
   Make 4
   Make 10

7. Making tumbling blocks: It is very important to keep the placement of the light, medium and dark fabric in the same position to get the 3-D effect. The light is on top, the medium is to the right and the dark is to the left.

8. Sew medium diamond to dark diamond. Use straight pins at the beginning and end to keep the seams together and to reduce stretching. Press seam toward the medium.

9. Lay the light diamond directly on top of the dark diamond. Check the alignment of the points. Pin the beginning and end to keep seams together and to reduce stretching. Sew the seam.

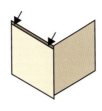

10. Unsew all stitching in the seam allowance. Try not to cut the thread just unstitch.

11. The last step is now a snap. Sew seam 3 to complete the tumbling block with a butterfly seam. Pin beginning and end of seam and edge to keep the folded diamond closed. Sew.

12. Unsew in the seam allowance and press toward dark diamond. Spin out the seam allowance from the back to form the cutest little tumbler. This is the key for a flat unit.

13. Make (18) tumbling blocks following the sketch and substituting "butterfly" diamond connectors when necessary.

14. Sew medium Polygon2 diamond to light Polygon2 pyramid to complete the left edge. Make (2).

15. Sew dark Polygon2 diamond to light Polygon2 pyramid to complete the right edge.

16. Layout tumbling blocks and edge blocks following sketch.

17. Sew tumbling blocks and edge blocks together to form rows.

18. Sew row to row using butterfly seams.

19. Inset the light Polygon2 pyramids and Polygon2 diamonds to the bottom of the quilt using butterfly seams. Trim edge straight.

20. Sew medium Polygon2 pyramid to dark Polygon2 pyramid. Make (3).

21. Inset to the top of the quilt using butterfly seams. Add Polygon2 pyramids to the top edge to complete the corners. Trim edge straight.

22. Layer backing, batting, and quilt top. Quilt as desired. This wallhanging speaks modern. Beth convinced me to try this wave pattern and it's perfect. Another idea is to hand big stitch the waves using #8 perle cotton.

23. Make binding by connecting (5) 2½" x 40" strips end to end. Fold and press in half lengthwise for a double binding. Sew binding to quilt.

24. Make a label to identify this quilt as being your art. Add a hanging sleeve and enjoy.

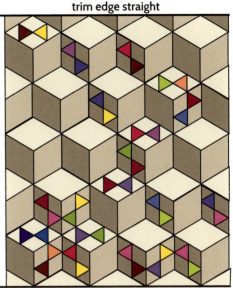

trim edge straight

trim edge straight

Nuts

I must be Nuts! But it's so much fun to gather charm diamonds. Nuts is made using Polygon diamonds. And yes, no fabric is repeated which means 813 different fabrics are used. Whew! And they all came from my stash. Spread the love by starting a charm club to collect either 5½" diamonds or 3" diamonds.

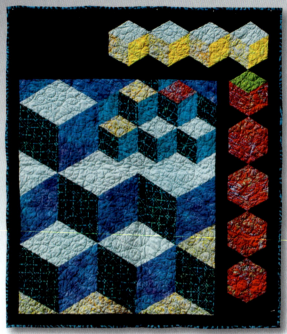

Picking Up the Pieces
32" x 36"
Kathy McLaren

*When Hexagons Get Together...
They See Stars*
98" x 90"
Mary Jo Yackley

*Modern Madrona Polygon
Double Diamonds*
20" x 20"
Charlotte Noll

POLYGON AFFAIR ENGAGED

Poly Dots
39" x 45"
Deborah Brobst

Line Dancing
48" x 52"
Gyleen X. Fitzgerald

Sunny Turquoise
41" x 29"
Caroline Frey
Mounvier-Vehier

All the Girls are Stars
71" x 80"
Carol Hansen

POLYGON AFFAIR — ENGAGED

Put a Ring on It
53" x 57"
Gyleen X. Fitzgerald
Quilted by Beth Hanlon-Ridder

PATTERN

Put a Ring on It

I will admit, some want the ring and some don't. In my mind there comes a time to fish or cut bait. Make sure you are at the right pond when fishing for your soulmate. If you are at the right pond, there will be lots of fish! When people are serious, they don't fish around; they focus on catching. When they are not serious, you, being hopeful, can hang on to the bait too long. I'm positive the perfect soulmate is busy catching you before you can say, "Put a ring on it." Diamonds, big or small, oh how I love how they sparkle.

Polygon Tool	Diamond
Polygon2 Tool	Pyramid
Block Size	10" x 11½"
Block Count	20

Supplies

(20) 3" x 40" strips, assorted fabric
½ yard for white diamonds
1 yard for connector diamond fabric
¾ yard for border
½ yard for binding

Instructions

1. From the assorted 3" strips, cross cut using Polygon Tool, (8) Polygon diamonds and (4) Polygon pyramids.

2. Using the white diamond fabric, cut (4) 3" x 40" strips. Cross cut into (40) Polygon diamonds.

3. Each diamond hexagon uses 3 fabrics; (6) polygon diamonds from fabric 1; (4) Polygon pyramids and (2) Polygon diamonds from fabric 2; and (2) white Polygon diamonds. Sort for (20) sets.

4. Using a set, sew fabric 1 diamond to fabric 2 diamond. Make (2).

5. Sew 2 together to make a 4-patch diamond. Press seam open.

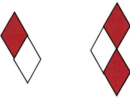

6. Sew a fabric 1 diamond to fabric 2 pyramid. Make mirror image as well.

7. Stitch to the bottom of 4-patch diamond. See sketch.

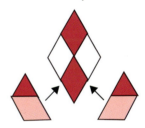

8. Sew fabric 1 diamond to fabric 2 pyramid to fabric 1 diamond. Make (2) and stitch to both sides of the diamond assembly to complete the Diamond Hexagon. See sketch.

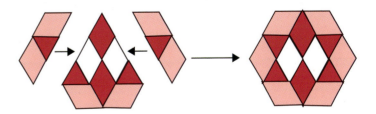

9. Repeat steps 4-8 using different fabric 1 and fabric 2 combinations, making (20) total Diamond Hexagons.

10. Layout blocks in (4) columns. Sew (5) Diamond Hexagon blocks end to end to complete the column. Repeat (3) times.

11. Cut (5) 5½" x 40" strips of diamond connector fabric. Cross cut (20) Polygon2 diamonds and (10) Polygon2 pyramids using Polygon2 Tool.

12. Insert Polygon2 diamonds to the column using a butterfly seam, following sketch for placement.

13. Add Polygon2 pyramids to the beginning and ending of columns, following sketch for placement.

14. Connect the columns using a butterfly seam.

15. Trim diamonds and pyramids for a straight edge and leaving ¼" seam allowance.

16. Using border fabric, cut (6) 3½" x 40" strips and sew end to end.

17. Measure quilt from top to bottom; cross cut (2) border strips to this length and stitch to the sides of the quilt. Press seams toward border.

18. Measure quilt from side to side; cross cut (2) border strips to this length and stitch to top and bottom of quilt. Press seams toward border.

19. Layer backing, batting, and quilt top. Baste layers together. Quilt as desired. The sample is quilted with watermelon red cotton thread using a longarm sewing machine and contains a stylized swirly heart pattern.

20. Using binding fabric, cut (6) 2½" x 40" strip and sew end to end. Fold lengthwise and press for a double fold binding. Sew to quilt.

21. Make a label to identify this quilt as being your art and enjoy.

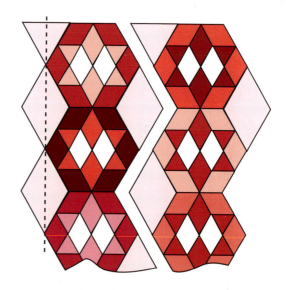

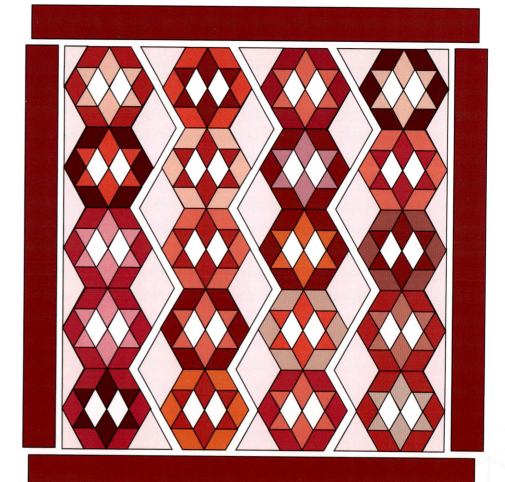

Something Old–Something New
45" x 39"
Barbara Herron

PATTERN

Something Old…Something New

Barbara Herron, a collector of antique linen, quilt blocks and tops made the best of what otherwise might have been discarded. She fussy cut Polygon2 hexagons to save hand embroidery or motifs. Her pathway diamonds and pyramids were cut from feedsacks in honor of her traditional roots. Barbara used the Begonia Flower; however, any of the Flower Girl designs (shown on page 120) can be used in this project. Take advantage of vintage linen and watch it be transformed into a delicate garden table cloth.

Polygon Tool	Diamond & Pyramid
Polygon2 Tool	Hexagon
Block Size	15" x 15"
Block Count	7

Supplies

(7) 5½" x 40" strips for flowers
(2) 5½" x 40" strips for flower centers
(4) 3" x 40" strips for pathway
½ yard for binding

Instructions

1. Using (7) flower strips and Polygon2 Tool, open strip to one layer and cut (6) Polygon2 diamonds then cross cut into Polygon2 hexagons.

2. Using flower center fabric strips, open strips to one layer and cut (7) Polygon2 diamonds. Cross cut (7) Polygon2 hexagons.

3. Lay out the flower using (6) flowers hexagons and (1) center hexagon; sew a "ring" of flower hexagons first (all but the last seam to close the ring). Then start doing the butterfly seam to insert the center hexagon. The last seam is to close the ring.

4. Make (7) Begonia Flowers.

5. Using the pathway strips and Polygon Tool, cut (30) Polygon diamonds. Insert one diamond to each flower using the butterfly seam. See sketch.

6. Using the pathway strips and Polygon Tool, cut (12) Polygon pyramids. Sew (2) pyramids to each flower. See sketch.

Note: They will be on the opposite side of the pathway diamond.

Connect flower to flower using butterfly seam

7. Sew flowers together to form rows using a butterfly seam. Make (3) rows of 2, 3, and 2 flowers.

8. Insert pathway diamonds between the flower hexagons on one side of flower row using a butterfly seam. Following sketch, note the location of PARTIAL seams.

9. Connect the rows. row to row using butterfly seams, following the stitching order on the sketch. Then complete partial seam.

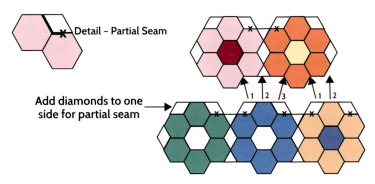

10. The table cloth finishes in a hexagon shape. Using the remainder of the 3" pathway strip and the Polygon2 Tool, position the hexagon and pyramid marks between the top and bottom of the strip. Cut (6) half hexagons.

11. Add Polygon2 half hexagons and add or remove pyramids or diamonds to complete the straight edge.

12. Layer backing, batting, and quilt top. Quilt as desired. Barbara big stitched the table cloth using #8 perle cotton.

13. Using binding fabric, cut (4) 2½" x 40" strips and sew end to end. Press strip in half lengthwise for a double binding. Sew binding to quilt.

14. Make a label to identify this quilt as being your art and enjoy.

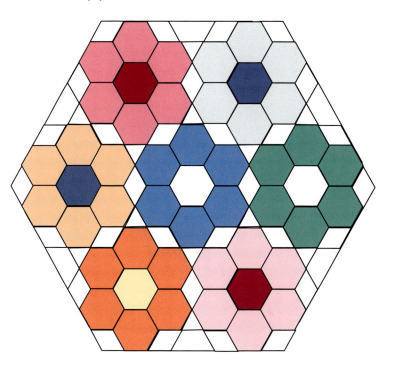

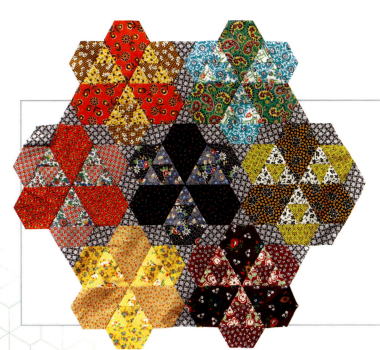

Mae's Trillium Garden

Keeping the theme Something Old… Something New, I started Mae's Trillium Garden as a tribute to the collection of original 1920's vintage fabric I inherited from Betty Phelps. Mae was her mother-in-law and I now have what remains of her stash. I used Trillium from the Flower Girl blocks (page 120) and purchased the black and white print fabric for the pathway. My plan is to grow this into a bed quilt so I can document as much of her stash as possible.

Bottoms Up
62" x 62"
Gyleen X. Fitzgerald
Quilted by Beth Hanlon-Ridder

PATTERN

Bottom's Up

Cheers! Stacked, the dark pyramids are filled and stacked, the light pyramids are empty. No drinking while quilting and certainly no drinking while driving. Here! Here! Bottom's Up to the groom and his men.

Polygon Tool	Diamond & Pyramid
Polygon2 Tool	Diamond & Pyramid
Block Size	10" x 11½"
Block Count	30

Supplies

(11) 3" x 40" strips, assorted light fabric
(11) 3" x 40" strips, assorted dark fabric
(9) 22" x 18" assorted fabric for background
1 yard for border
½ yard for binding

Instructions

1. From the assorted 3" strips both light and dark, cross cut using Polygon Tool as many Polygon pyramids as possible. Each block uses (6) light and (6) dark pyramids.

2. Using the background fabric, cut (4) 3" x 22" strips. Crosscut into (24) Polygon diamonds per fabric. Each block uses (6) diamonds.

3. Using the remaining of the background fabrics cut 5½" x 22" strips. Cross cut (10) Polygon2 diamonds and (8) Polygon2 pyramids with the Polygon2 Tool.

4. Sort shapes into sets using only (3) fabrics per block; make (30) block sets with (6) light and (6) dark pyramids and (6) diamonds.

5. Using a set, sew light pyramid to dark pyramid to light pyramid. Make (3).

6. Layout assemblies per sketch and sew together using a butterfly seam.

7. Sew a background diamond to dark pyramid to background diamond per sketch. Make (3).

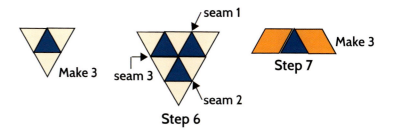

8. Sew to pyramid assembly of step 6. Press seams away from center. See sketch.

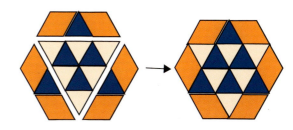

9. Repeat step 5-8, making (30) hexagon blocks.

10. Layout blocks in (6) columns. Sew (5) hexagon blocks end to end to complete the column. Repeat (5) times.

11. Make filler pieced half hexagons to complete top or bottom of columns. For the bottom of columns select (3) dark pyramids and (1) light pyramid. Sew together to form a pieced pyramid. Make (6).

Bottom Edge - Make 6

12. Sew pieced pyramid to background Polygon2 pyramid to pieced pyramid. Make (3).

13. Add to the bottom of columns 2, 4 and 6.

14. For the top of the columns select (3) light pyramids and (1) dark pyramid. Sew together to form a pieced pyramid. Make (6).

15. Sew pieced pyramid to background Polygon2 pyramid to pieced pyramid. Make (3).

Top Edge - Make 3

16. Add to the top of columns 1, 3 and 5.

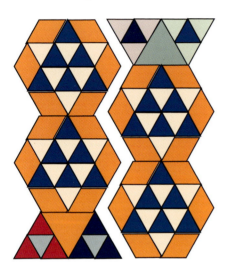

17. Connect the column to column using a butterfly seam. See sketch.

18. For the side edges, add background Polygon2 diamonds between the hexagon blocks using a butterfly seam and add background Polygon2 pyramids to corners.

19. Trim diamonds and pyramids for a straight edge and leaving a ¼" seam allowance.

20. Using border fabric, cut (7) 4" x 40" strips and sew end to end.

21. Measure quilt from top to bottom; cross cut (2) border strips to this length and stitch to the sides of the quilt. Press seams toward border.

22. Measure quilt from side to side; cross cut (2) border strips to this length and stitch to top and bottom of quilt. Press seams toward border.

23. Layer backing, batting, and quilt top. Baste layers together. Quilt as desired. The sample is quilted with lime thread using a loopy bubble pattern.

24. Using binding fabric, cut (7) 2½" x 40" strip and sew end to end. Fold lengthwise and press for a double fold binding. Sew to quilt.

25. Make a label to identify this quilt as being your art and enjoy.

In quilting, just as in life, I love a challenge!

My first guild challenge was with Mountain Laurel Quilt Guild in Wellsboro, Pennsylvania in the summer of 2013. The rules were as follows:

CHALLENGE RULES

1. A recognizable amount of the "Ribbit Stripe" by Alexander Henry Fabrics Collection (obtained from Needles Quilt Shop) must be used as an integral part of the entry and must appear in the body of the quilt, not just the border. Any amount of any other fabric may be used.

2. The **Polygon2 Tool by Gyleen** must be used in the making of the quilt top. All shapes from the tool can be used (hexagon, pyramid, diamond, cone). Other shapes may be combined in the quilt, however, the shapes from Polygon2 must dominate.

3. The quilt can be of any shape. While a non-traditional shape is acceptable, if selected as the winner, your completed quilt must hang well from a sleeve with no other support or pins.

4. Judging emphasizes originality, creative use of the challenge fabric as it relates to other fabrics, visual impact, and workmanship.

And the winners...

Diamonds and Stripes
41" x 48"
Betty Maxwell

Zig Zag Beach
51" x 59"
Kathleen Plumley

Sunshine Circus
52" x 58"
Deborah Dorn

Waltz with Me
70" x 80"
Gyleen X. Fitzgerald
Quilted by Beth Hanlon-Ridder

PATTERN

Waltz With Me

Shall we dance? Soft and delicate with a swing and turn, that's what I feel with following Pyramid Stars. Mothers have so many proud moments but few can compare to the dance they will have with their sons. Perhaps her last dance before she lets him go to his new wife. Bitter and sweet, her boy has become a man. Waltz with Me, soft and delicate with a swing and a turn.

Polygon Tool	Diamond
Polygon2 Tool	Pyramid
Block Size	10" x 11½"
Block Count	28

Supplies

(14) 22" x 18" star feature fabric
1 yard black for block and border 1
1½ yards white for block
¼ yard for border 2
¼ yard for binding

Instructions

1. Using a feature fabric, cut (1) 3" x 22" strip, cross cut (6) Polygon diamonds using the Polygon Tool and cut (1) 5½" x 22" strip, cross cut (3) Polygon2 pyramids using the Polygon2 Tool. Repeat for each feature fabric.

2. Using the black fabric, cut (8) 3" x 40" strips. Cross cut into as many Polygon diamonds as possible using the Polygon Tool. Cut more as needed.

3. Using white fabric cut (14) 3" x 40" strips. Cross cut into as many Polygon diamonds as possible using the Polygon Tool. Cut more as needed.

4. Sort into Star sets: (3) diamonds from one feature fabric, (3) black diamonds and (6) white diamonds. Make (28) sets.

5. Using one set, lay pieces (one feature, one black and one white diamond) per the sketch to form a tumbling block.

6. Sew tumbling blocks together using a butterfly seam. Make (3), keeping orientation of the diamonds the same block to block. See Sketch.

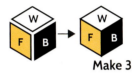

Make 3

7. Position the (3) blocks so that the white diamond is to the outside. See sketch.

8. Inset (3) white diamonds using a butterfly seam between the remaining star points to complete the pieced star block. See sketch.

10. Using the (3) Polygon2 pyramids that match the feature fabric, sew to side of the pieced star block that has a black diamond to complete the large pyramid star block. See sketch.

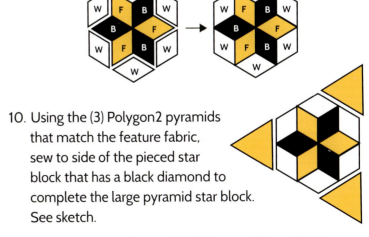

11. Repeat steps 5-10 to make (28) pyramid star blocks.

12. Begin to layout the pyramid stars into (4) columns containing (7) pyramid stars following sketch. Join block to block to form the column.

13. Make partial pyramid stars for top and bottom of columns. Each partial pyramid star requires (3) white diamonds, (2) black diamonds, (2) feature fabric diamonds and (2) feature fabric Polygon2 pyramids. Cut more shapes from remaining 3" and 5½" strips.

14. Layout a tumbling blocks per sketch. Sew together with a butterfly seam. Make (2).

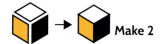
Make 2

15. Sew tumbling blocks together per sketch. Be mindful of orientation.

16. Add a white diamond between feature fabric and black diamond.

17. Sew Polygon2 pyramids to side with black diamond for bottom of columns 1 & 3 and top of 2 & 4. See sketch.

Step 15   Step 16   Step 17   Make 4

18. Repeat steps 13-17 for (4) right partial pyramid stars.

19. Sew to top of columns 2 & 4 and the bottom of columns 1 & 3.

20. Make mirror image partial pyramid stars using (3) white diamonds, (2) black diamonds, (2) feature fabric diamonds and (2) feature fabric Polygon2 pyramids. Cut more shapes if necessary.

Columns 1 & 3   **Columns 2 & 4**

21. Following sketch, layout tumbling block and note the orientation is reversed. Sew together using a butterfly seam. Make (2).

22. Sew tumbling block together per sketch.

23. Add white diamond between black and feature fabric diamonds.

24. Sew Polygon2 pyramids to side with black diamonds for bottom of columns 2 & 4 and top of 1 & 3. See sketch.

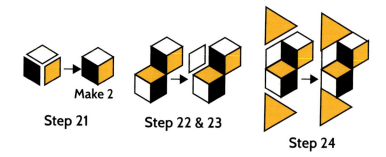
Step 21   Step 22 & 23   Step 24
Make 2

25. Repeat steps 20-24 for (4) left partial pyramid stars.

26. Sew to top of columns 1 & 3 and bottom of columns 2 & 4.

27. Sew the (4) columns together to form the quilt top.

28. Trim top and bottom of finished quilt for a straight edge, making sure to leave a ¼" seam allowance.

29. Using border 1 fabric, cut (7) 2" x 40" strips and sew end to end.

30. Measure quilt from top to bottom; cross cut (2) border strips to this length and stitch to the sides of the quilt. Press seams toward border.

31. Measure quilt from side to side; cross cut (2) border strips to this length and stitch to top and bottom of quilt. Press seams toward border.

32. Using border 2 fabric, cut (7) 3½" x 40" strips and sew end to end.

33. Measure quilt from top to bottom; cross cut (2) border strips to this length and stitch to the sides of the quilt. Press seams toward border.

POLYGON AFFAIR   THE MOTHER'S DANCE

34. Measure quilt from side to side; cross cut (2) border strips to this length and stitch to top and bottom of quilt. Press seams toward border.

35. Layer backing, batting, and quilt top. Baste layers together. Quilt as desired.

36. Using binding fabric, cut (7) 2½" x 40" strip and sew end to end. Fold lengthwise and press for a double fold binding. Sew to quilt.

37. Make a label to identify this quilt as being your art and enjoy.

POLYGON AFFAIR   THE MOTHER'S DANCE

Harlequin Christmas
38" x 46"
Peg Dougherty

PATTERN

Party Favors

I read, on the internet of course, that five Jordan almonds given to wedding guests in a confection box or wrapped in elegant fabric is the classic party favor. The covered almonds symbolize fertility, longevity, wealth, health, and happiness. Peg's Ice Floes (page 17, upper right) keeps the design modern for today's bride by using clear, crisp colors. Whatever the occasion, everybody likes a little something to remember the day.

Polygon Tool	Diamond & Pyramid
Polygon2 Tool	Diamond & Pyramid
Block Size	20" x 10"
Block Count	16

Supplies

½ yard for center fabric
½ yard of fabric A
½ yard of fabric B
½ yard of fabric C
½ yard of fabric D
½ yard for binding

Instructions

1. Using the center fabric, cut (3) 5½" x 40" strips, cross cut (13) Polygon2 diamonds and (10) Polygon2 pyramids using the Polygon2 Tool.

2. Cut (4) 3" x 40" strips from fabric A, B, C, and D.

3. Using fabric A, cross cut (16) Polygon diamonds using Polygon Tool. Using fabric C, cross cut (8) Polygon diamonds and (16) Polygon pyramids using the Polygon Tool.

4. Layer fabric A and B strips, right sides together and sew together, using ¼" seam, lengthwise on both sides. See Sketch.

5. Using the Polygon Tool, cut (20) Polygon pyramids.

6. You will have stitching on two sides of the cut pyramid. Remove the stitching across the point. Open assembly and press seam to the darker pyramid.

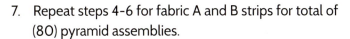

7. Repeat steps 4-6 for fabric A and B strips for total of (80) pyramid assemblies.

8. Using fabric A/B pyramid assembly, sew (2) together and add to the lower right side of the center Polygon2 diamond.

9. Sew (3) pyramids assemblies together, sew to lower left side of center Polygon2 diamond.

10. Sew fabric A Polygon diamond to (2) pyramid assemblies sewn together. Sew to upper left side of center Polygon2 diamond.

Step 8

Step 9

Step 10

POLYGON AFFAIR   97   THE MOTHER'S DANCE

11. Sew (3) pyramid assemblies together then add fabric A diamond. Sew to upper right side of center Polygon2 diamond to complete the Party Favors block.

12. Make (8) A/B Party Favors blocks.

13. Layer fabric C and D strips, right sides together and sew together, using ¼" seam, lengthwise on both sides. Repeat steps 5 and 6 for a total of (84) pyramid assemblies.

14. Using C/D pyramid assembly, repeat steps 8-12 to make (3) C/D Party Favors blocks.

15. Using fabric C and D, sew fabric C pyramid to (2) fabric C/D pyramid assemblies. Sew to the left side of center Polygon2 pyramid.

16. Sew (3) C/D pyramid assemblies to fabric C pyramid. Sew to the right side of center Polygon2 pyramid to complete the half-Party Favor block.

Step 11

Step 12

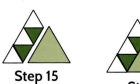
Step 15   Step 16

17. Make (6) C/D half-Party Favor blocks for top and bottom.

18. Make (2) left and (2) right C/D partial half-Party Favor blocks by sewing (3) C/D pyramid assemblies to fabric C pyramid and adding to the left or right side of central fabric Polygon2 pyramid.

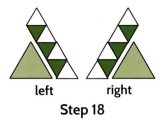
left   right
Step 18

19. Make C/D side assemblies by sewing (3) C/D pyramid assemblies together then sew to bottom left of center Polygon2 diamond.

20. Sew (3) C/D pyramid assemblies together then add fabric C diamond. Add to upper left side of center Polygon2 diamond. Make (2) side assemblies.

21. Layout out Party Favor blocks and sew together to form diagonal rows.

22. Sew row to row then trim edge straight.

23. Layer backing, batting, and quilt top. Baste layers together. Quilt as desired. A simple edge to edge pattern or grid would be perfect or big stitch using #8 perle cotton.

24. Using binding fabric, cut (5) 2½" x 40" strips and sew end to end. Fold lengthwise and press for a double fold binding. Sew to quilt.

25. Make a label to identify this quilt as being your art, add hanging sleeve and enjoy.

Step 19

Step 20

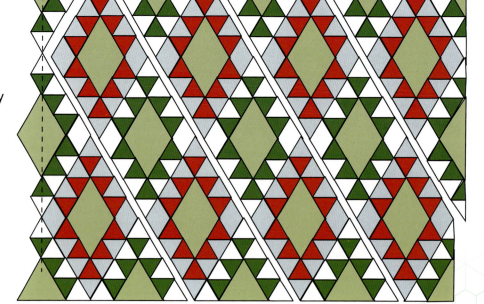

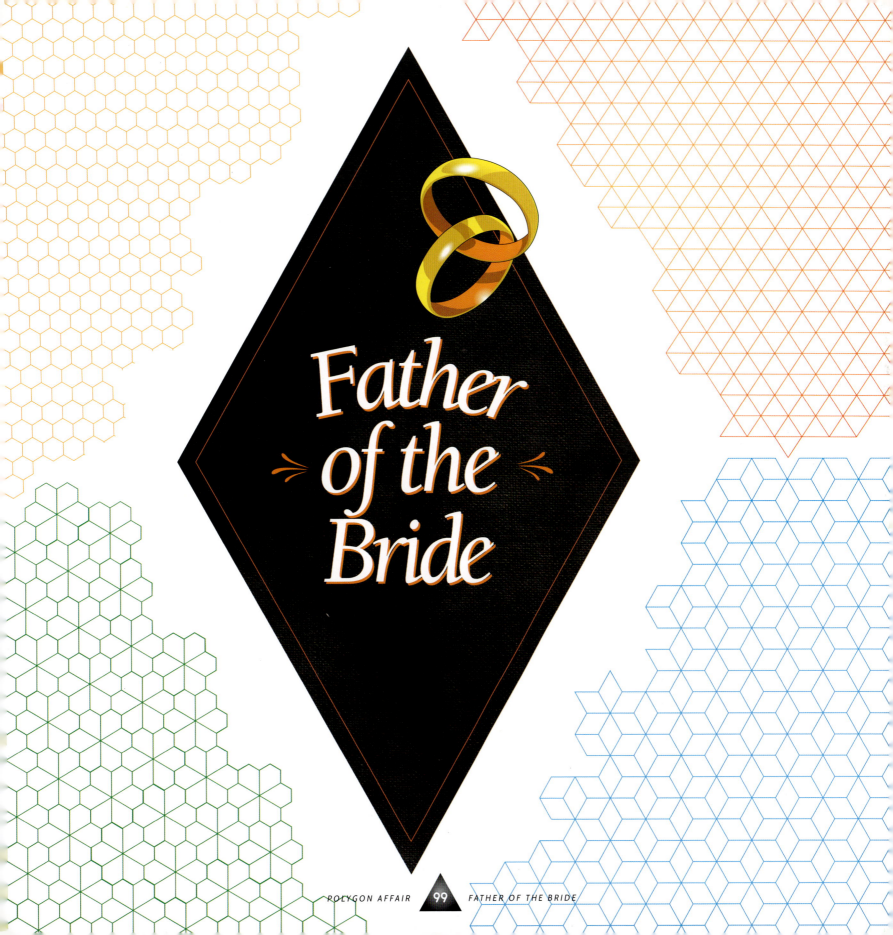

Father of the Bride
47" x 41"
Gyleen X. Fitzgerald
Quilted by Beth Hanlon-Ridder

PATTERN

Father of the Bride

Fathers are excited, nervous, and protective on the day of their little girl's wedding. They have the tremendous duty of escorting the bride to her groom. They pass the baton of expectations, man to man. For me, hero is the first thing that comes to mind when I think of my father. What I saw in him set the bar for the man I would marry. This is my salute to the men, the heroes in life.

Polygon Tool	Pyramid
Polygon2 Tool	Cone
Block Size	11" x 5"

Supplies

1 yard of fabric A
1 yard of fabric B
1 yard of fabric C
(10) assorted 3" x 22" strips for accent pyramids
½ yard for binding

Instructions

1. Using fabrics A, B, and C, cut (4) 5½" x 40" strips, cut (23) Polygon2 diamonds and cross cut into Polygon2 cones using the Polygon2 Tool.

2. Using the 3" x 22" strips, cut an assortment of (69) pyramids using Polygon Tool.

3. Sew a pyramid to the tip of each cone. See sketch.

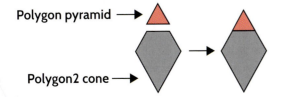

4. Layout pieced cones per sketch. I spent more time designing the layout than I did piecing the cones. This can be a very modern quilt so consider designing your own layout; take your time and enjoy the process.

5. Sew together to form diagonal rows.

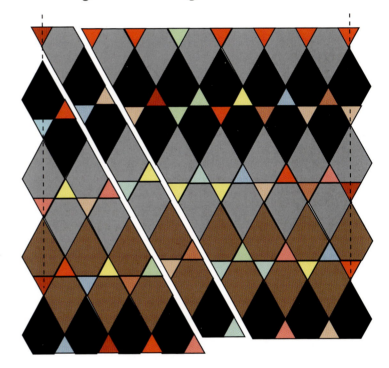

6. Sew row to row then trim edge straight.

7. Layer backing, batting, and quilt top. Baste layers together. Quilt as desired. A simple edge to edge pattern or grid would be perfect or big stitch using #8 perle cotton.

8. Using binding fabric, cut (4) 2½" x 40" strips and sew end-to-end. Fold lengthwise and press for a double fold binding. Sew to quilt.

9. Make a label to identify this quilt as being your art, add hanging sleeve and enjoy.

POLYGON AFFAIR   101   FATHER OF THE BRIDE

Rocket's Red Glare (Soldier's Quilt)
62" x 66"
Carol Hansen

PATTERN

Rocket's Red Glare

Red, white and blue – quilters have been making star quilts in our country's colors since Betsy Ross stitched our first flag. It's a classic on most quilter's "must do" list. I designed Rocket's Red Glare as a salute to our wounded warriors. Be inspired to make a soldier's quilt using this or any of the star blocks presented in Polygon Affair. Special thanks to Carol for doing just that.

Polygon Tool	Pyramid
Polygon2 Tool	Diamond & Pyramid
Block Size	23" x 20"
Block Count	6

Supplies

(6) red fabrics – ⅓ yard each
(6) blue fabrics – ½ yard each
(6) white fabrics – ¼ yard each
1 yard for border 1 and binding
¾ yard for border 2

Instructions

1. Using (1) red fabric, cut (1) 5½" x 40" strip; cross cut (3) Polygon2 diamonds and (3) Polygon2 pyramids using the Polygon2 Tool.

2. Using (1) blue fabric, cut (1) 5½" x 40" strip; cross cut (6) Polygon2 diamonds using the Polygon2 Tool.

3. Using (1) white fabric, cut (1) 5½" x 40" strip; cross cut (3) Polygon2 pyramids using the Polygon2 Tool.

4. Sew one red diamond to one white pyramid. Make (3). See sketch.

5. Sew the (3) assemblies together forming a large pyramid using a butterfly seam. See sketch.

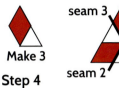
Make 3
Step 4

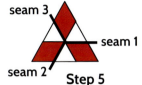
seam 3
seam 1
seam 2
Step 5

6. Sew one blue diamond to a red pyramid to a blue diamond. Make (3). See sketch.

7. Sew assembly to each side of the large pyramid to form one star block.

Make 3
Step 6

Step 7

8. Repeat steps 1-7 to make a total of (6) star blocks.

9. Using (1) red fabric, cut (1) 5½" x 40" strip; cross cut (3) Polygon2 pyramids using the Polygon2 Tool.

10. Using (1) blue fabric, cut (1) 3" x 40" strip; cross cut (1) Polygon pyramid using the Polygon Tool.

11. Using (1) white fabric, cut (1) 3" x 40" strip; cross cut (3) Polygon pyramids using the Polygon Tool.

12. Layout pyramid connector. See sketch.

13. Starting with the blue pyramid, add white pyramid to each side then add red pyramid to each side. Press seam after each addition.

Make 6

POLYGON AFFAIR — FATHER OF THE BRIDE

14. Repeat steps 9-13 to make a total of (6) pyramid connectors.

15. Sew one pyramid connector to a star block (once sewn, looks like a cone shape). Make (3) of one orientation and (3) of the other for (6) total. See Sketch.

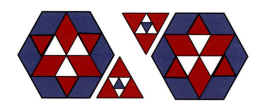

16. Position assembly and sew together per sketch to form rows. Make (3).

17. Sew row to row.

18. Using the remaining 5½" strips of red, white, or blue fabric and the Polygon2 Tool, cross cut (26) Polygon2 diamonds and (8) Polygon2 pyramids. Cut additional strips if necessary.

19. Following sketch, layout and sew the edge assemblies.

 Make 2   Make 2   Make 4

20. Sew the edge assemblies to both side of the quilt top following the stitching order on the sketch.

Quilts for Heroes

Carol Sue Hansen felt a need to do something to honor her husband, father, and father-in-law. Her father-in-law served in WWII and earned two Purple Hearts. Her passion is for Quilts for Heroes.

Quilts for Heroes is a small group of dedicated quilters who meet every Monday evening on the post of Aberdeen Proving Ground in Maryland. They are one of about five small groups in Maryland that contribute to Quilts of Valor. Quilts for Heroes' mission is to make quilts and present them to warriors for comfort and to show appreciation for their service to our country.

Most of the members in Quilts for Heroes were federal employees who supported the military throughout their career. Many have a personal connection to the military, through a grandparent, parent, son, or daughter who served. Very few were quilters before joining. Working independently, their quilts meet the guidelines established by Quilts of Valor. Quilts for Heroes has presented nearly 700 quilts since its inception in 2004. They are dedicated to continue until all our wariors are home.

Carol Sue Hansen is the founder and CEO for Quilts for Heroes.

21. Trim diamonds for a straight edge.

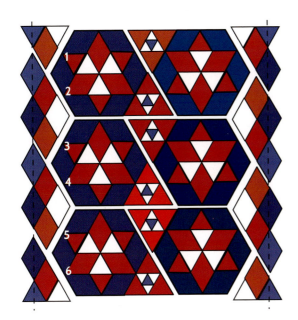

22. Using border 1 fabric, cut (6) 2½" x 40" strips and sew end to end.

23. Measure quilt from top to bottom; cross cut (2) border strips to this length and stitch to the sides of the quilt. Press seams toward border.

24. Measure quilt from side to side; cross cut (2) border strips to this length and stitch to top and bottom of quilt. Press seams toward border.

25. Using border 2 fabric, cut (7) 3½" x 40" strips and sew end to end.

26. Measure quilt from top to bottom; cross cut (2) border strips to this length and stitch to the sides of the quilt. Press seams toward border.

27. Measure quilt from side to side; cross cut (2) border strips to this length and stitch to top and bottom of quilt. Press seams toward border.

28. Layer backing, batting, and quilt top. Baste layers together. Quilt as desired; a star motif would be perfect.

29. Using binding fabric, cut (7) 2½" x 40" strips and sew end to end. Fold lengthwise and press for a double fold binding. Sew to quilt.

30. Make a label to identify this quilt as being your art and enjoy.

Note: Size requirements for Quilts of Valor is 55" – 77" wide by 65" – 90" long.

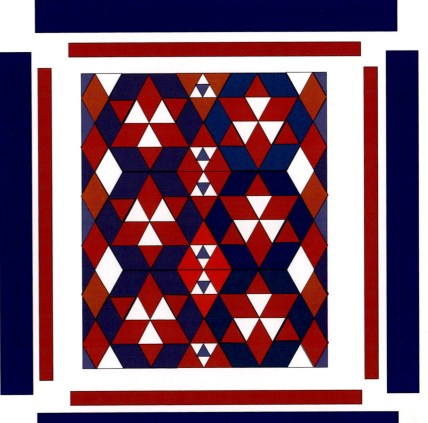

POLYGON AFFAIR   FATHER OF THE BRIDE

Two Become One
45" x 47"
Gyleen X. Fitzgerald
Quilted by Beth Hanlon-Ridder

PATTERN

Two Become One

"For this reason a man shall leave his father and mother and be joined to his wife, and the two shall become one flesh." —Ephesians 5:31

Polygon Tool	Diamond & Pyramid
Polygon2 Tool	Diamond & Pyramid
Block Size	23" x 20"
Block Count	4

Supplies

1 yard of small star background fabric
1 yard of large star background fabric and binding
½ yard of large star point fabric
22" x 18" feature fabric (soloist)
⅔ yard harmonizer fabric

Instructions

1. Using the soloist fabric, cut (3) 5½" x 40" strips, cut (5) Polygon2 hexagons, (6) Polygon2 pyramids and (2) Polygon2 diamonds with the Polygon2 Tool.

2. Using the small star background fabric, cut (5) 3" x 40" strips. Cross cut (32) Polygon diamonds and (8) Polygon pyramids. Cut (1) 5½" x 40" strips. Cross cut (10) Polygon2 pyramids.

3. Using the harmonizer, cut (5) 3" x 40" strips. Cross cut (34) Polygon pyramids.

4. Sew a harmonizer Polygon pyramid to every other side of the soloist Polygon2 hexagon to make a pieced pyramid. Press toward the hexagon. See sketch.

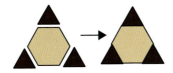

5. Sew a small star background Polygon diamond to harmonizer Polygon pyramid to a small star background Polygon diamond in a row. Press toward the diamond. Make (3). See sketch.

Make 3

6. Sew assembly to the sides of pieced small pyramid to complete a Lone Star block. Make (5).

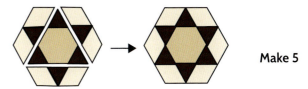

Make 5

7. Repeat Steps 4-6 using the Lone Star block instead of the hexagon. See Sketch. Make (4) Two Become One blocks.

Make 3

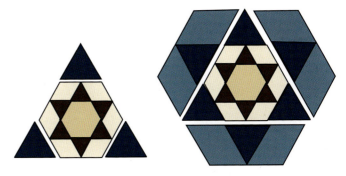

8. To the remaining Lone Star block, add Polygon2 pyramids (small star background fabric) to top and bottom. This is the center connector.

9. Layer 3" x 40" strips of small star background fabric and harmonizer fabric, right sides together and sew together, using ¼" seam, lengthwise on both sides. See Sketch.

10. Using the Polygon Tool, cut as many Polygon pyramids as possible.

11. Note that you will have stitching on two sides of the cut pyramid. Remove the stitching across the point. Open assembly and press seam to the darker pyramid.

12. Repeat steps 11-13 as needed to complete the design.

13. For the center half pyramid connectors, sew (2) pyramid assemblies together and add small star background pyramid. Sew to left side of soloist Polygon2 pyramid. See sketch.

14. Sew (3) pyramids assemblies together and add small star background pyramid. Sew to right side. See sketch. Make (2).

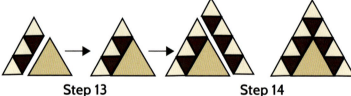

Step 13   Step 14

15. For the edge diamond connectors, sew a pyramid assembly to harmonizer Polygon pyramid. Add to top left side of soloist Polygon2 diamond.

16. Sew small star background diamond to pyramid assembly to harmonizer pyramid. Add to lower left side of soloist diamond. See sketch.

Step 16

17. Add small star background Polygon2 pyramid to each end of assembly. See sketch. Make (2).

18. For the corner partial pyramid connectors. Sew together (2) pyramid assemblies and add to the right side of soloist Polygon2 pyramid. Then add small star background Polygon2 pyramid to the top. Make (2) left and (2) right.

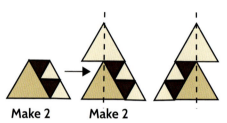

Make 2   Make 2

19. Sew (2) Two Become One blocks together to form 2 columns. Insert the center Lone Star connector using a butterfly seam to ONE column.

20. Sew the center half pyramid connectors to the top and bottom of the OTHER column.

21. Now you will have nice long seams to stitch. Join the two columns using butterfly seams.

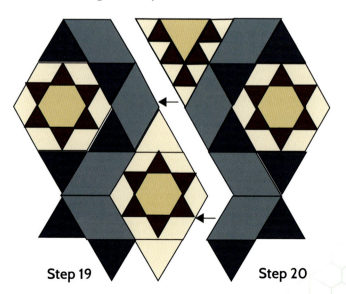

Step 19   Step 20

POLYGON AFFAIR   HAPPILY EVER AFTER

22. Now the side and corners. Add the edge diamond connector to the center left and right side using a butterfly seam.

23. Add the partial edge connections to the corners. Trim side edge straight.

24. For the pieced border, sew (16) pyramid assemblies together. Add one small star background pyramid to the end. Make (2).

25. Sew to top and bottom of the quilt. Trim corners for a straight edge, making sure to leave a ¼" seam allowance.

26. Layer backing, batting, and quilt top. Baste layers together. Quilt as desired.

27. Using binding fabric, cut (5) 2½" x 40" strips and sew end to end. Fold lengthwise and press for a double fold binding. Sew to quilt.

28. Make a label to identify this quilt as being your art, add hanging sleeve and enjoy.

Mardi Gras Stars
52" x 53"
Barbara O. Hudson

Two into One
46" x 46"
Vicki M. McCormick

*Iron Quilter Challenge–
Take Five Team*
40" x 70"
Gyleen X. Fitzgerald, Kathy Delorey,
Liz Rinda, Lynn Wannberg,
Carol Womack

Oh Happy Day
52" x 51"
Suzanna Foote

Bird in the Garden
47" x 40"
Virginia Hodge

Pursuit of Happiness
60" x 65"
Gyleen X. Fitzgerald
Quilted by Ashley Malinowski

PATTERN

Pursuit of Happiness

Is life ever perfect or is perfect what you make life to be? For me, quilting, love, and life are always evolving. Every day, I try to push the possibilities a little by pruning what isn't working and nurturing what needs to grow. I am in a constant quest for perfect balance.

Polygon Tool	Pyramid
Polygon2 Tool	Half Hexagon & Hexagon
Block Size	10" x 11½"
Block Count	26

Supplies

1 yard for center fabric
(15-16) 3" x 40" strips, assorted fabric for half hexagons
1 yard accent fabric for pyramids
2 yards striped border fabric
½ yard for binding

Instructions

1. Using the accent fabric, cut (8) 3" x 40" strips. Cross cut (50) Polygon pyramids with the Polygon Tool.

2. Using the 3" x 40" assorted strips cross cut as many Polygon2 half hexagons as possible with the Polygon2 Tool. Cut by placing the strip between the pyramid and hexagon marks on the Polygon2 Tool. Rotate tool upside down and repeat. Cut (156).

3. Using the center fabric, cut (5) 5½" x 40" strips. Cross cut (26) Polygon2 hexagons with the Polygon2 Tool.

4. Sew (6) half Hexagons together to form a ring. LEAVE THE LAST SEAM OPEN. Press seams to one side in the same direction.

5. Sew center hexagon to half Hexagon ring using a butterfly seam. The last seam should be to close the half Hexagon ring. Make a few or make (26) Happiness blocks.

6. Sew pyramid to side of the Happiness block. This is going to be a partial seam; start at the halfway point and end at the edge of the Happiness block. See sketch.

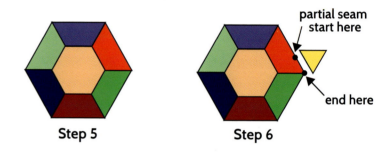

Step 5   Step 6

7. Repeat to make a second Happiness block.

8. Sew the two assemblies together with a complete end to end seam. Note that the partial seams are still hanging. See sketch.

9. Make another Happiness block. Add accent pyramid with partial seam.

10. Position to nest within the assembly. Sew complete end to end seam. See sketch.

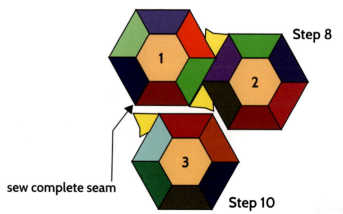

POLYGON AFFAIR   114   HAPPILY EVER AFTER

11. Add pyramid with a partial seam to other side of Happiness block 2.

12. Now complete the end to end seam between block 2 and 3.

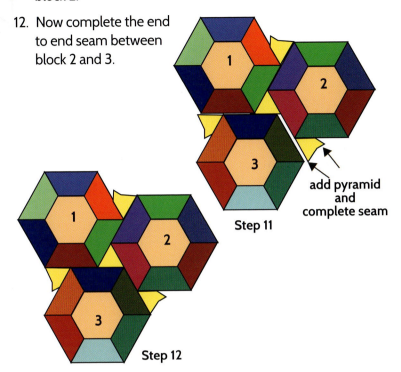

Step 11

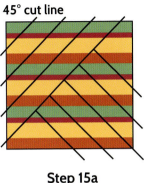

add pyramid and complete seam

Step 12

13. To continue the assembly, repeat steps 9-12. You will always need to add a pyramid with partial seam to a Happiness block. Once the pyramid is attached, you will have an end to end straight seam to stitch. Then check to see if just adding another pyramid with partial seam will complete another end to end straight seam.

Note: This is harder to write than it is to just do it. Pursuit of Happiness is a very organic quilt so you can add Happiness blocks in any direction and as many as you like. It's best to add the blocks as you make them; there is no need to wait until all blocks are made.

For the background, my initial concept was to use a wide striped fabric with an overlay of flowers. I couldn't find anything in my stash that would work. Plan B was to go shopping. I purchased a narrow stripe and decided to cut it so the stripes, when cut in strips and sewn together, would form chevrons.

14. Using the border fabric cut fabric into 3" strips. If using a print, cut across fabric selvage to selvage.

15. If using a stripe that runs selvage to selvage or down the selvage, open fabric and cut on a 45° angle. Cross cut into 3" strips in both directions following diagram.

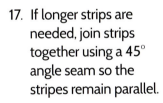

Step 15a   Step 15b

16. If using a diagonal stripe cut 3" strips both across the fabric and down the selvage. See sketch.

17. If longer strips are needed, join strips together using a 45° angle seam so the stripes remain parallel.

18. Alternate the strips to make the chevron pattern. See sketch.

19. Use the Polygon Tool to cut the end of the strip 60° before attaching to the quilt.

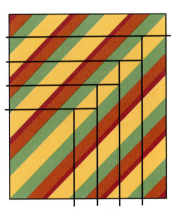

Step 16

Step 18

POLYGON AFFAIR   115   HAPPILY EVER AFTER

20. Starting at upper left edge of the of the Happiness quilt, roughly measure from last Happiness block to where you want the top of the quilt. Cut a 3" background strip to this length.

21. Sew strip to pyramid with a partial seam then complete the seam to attach to the Happiness block. Sew background strip to the quilt stopping about 1½" from end for a partial seam.

22. Select another background strip (with stripes going in the opposite direction). Measure the next length of background strip needed to where you want the top of the quilt. Cut a 3" background strip to this length. Cut the end to the angle using the Polygon Tool.

23. Add strip to pyramid with a partial seam. Then complete the seam between background strips. Pin, pin and pin AND always sew in the same direction. This will keep the edges from stretching.

24. Continue until the background is complete. Note that you may need to sew sets of background strips together first before adding to the Happiness quilt.

    Sometimes you are just adding a strip and at times a "set of strips". However each completes a partial seam in the quilt and with patience this goes very fast.

25. Repeat steps 20-24 for the bottom left edge of quilt.

26. Trim top and bottom of the quilt straight.

27. Layer backing, batting, and quilt top. Baste layers together. Quilt as desired. Ashley selected a huge hexagon pattern for the quilting and used a deep yellow thread.

28. Using binding fabric, cut (6) 2½" x 40" strips and sew end to end. Fold lengthwise and press for a double fold binding. Sew to quilt.

29. Make a label to identify this quilt as being your art and enjoy.

    Again, this concept of making chevrons and strip piecing the background is harder to explain than it is to do. Don't be afraid to pursue happiness!

POLYGON AFFAIR — HAPPILY EVER AFTER

Pursuit of Happiness
59" x 79"
Deborah Brobst

Wild Thing
53" x 62"
Nancy St. Pierre

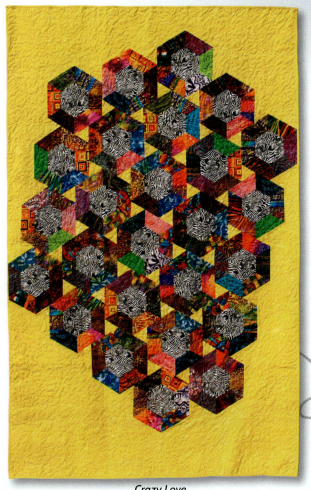

Crazy Love
79" x 51"
Gail E. Cooper Milburn

POLYGON AFFAIR HAPPILY EVER AFTER

Happiness Found on the Sun-Dappled Grand
52" x 73"
Lynn Van Keuren

Reflections from a Golden Eye
63" x 74"
Suzanna Foote

Universal Truth
78" x 71"
Kathy McLaren

POLYGON AFFAIR 118 HAPPILY EVER AFTER

Endless Love
Polymates...Blocks & Connectors

Oh, the possibilities! Be inspired to create your kind of love by replacing any of the blocks or connectors in my designs with any one of these for a totally fresh look. I've made the system easy. Here's is how it works.

The Polygon2 Hexagon Blocks are called 4x meaning their side length is four times the side length of the Polygon Tool. Armed with that knowledge, you can be play matchmaker by teaming them with any of the Connector–4x. The Polygon Hexagon Blocks which are 2x become a marriage made in heaven with Connector–2x.

The Flower Girls are 1x blocks. They like to play together. Use them for a contemporary look by connecting them block to block for Grandmother's Flower Garden. Or, simply convert the Flower Girls to Hexagon Blocks–3x by adding Polygon Diamonds; Connector–3x would be their perfect Polymate.

Love is in the air and my heart is fluttering!

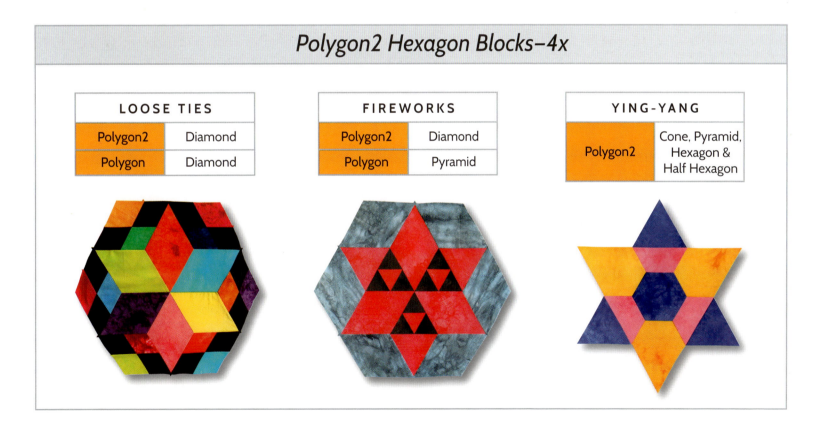

Polygon Hexagon Blocks–2x

BABY MAKES THREE

Polygon	Diamond & Pyramid

LONE STAR

Polygon	Diamond & Pyramid
Polygon2	Hexagon

DANCE ALL NIGHT

Polygon	Diamond & Pyramid
Polygon2	Hexagon

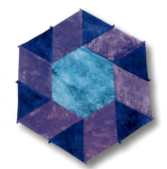

SEEING STARS

Polygon	Pyramid, Cone & Hexagon
Polygon2	Cone & Half Hexagon

Flower Girls–1x

IMPATIENS

Polygon2	Cone

ZINNIA

Polygon	Pyramid
Polygon2	Hexagon

VIOLET

Polygon	Pyramid
Polygon2	Hexagon & Cone

TRILLIUM

Polygon	Pyramid
Polygon2	Cone & Half Hexagon

BEGONIA

Polygon2	Hexagon

POLYGON AFFAIR · ENDLESS LOVE

Connectors–2x

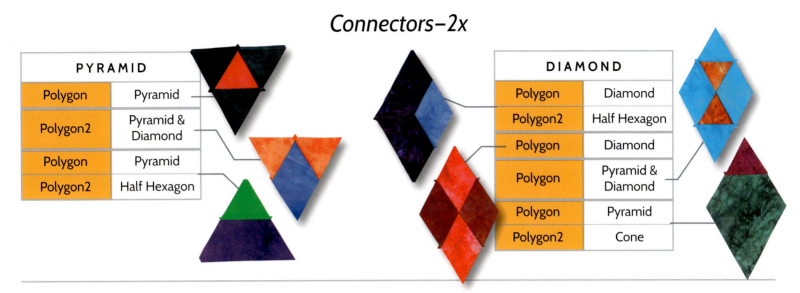

Connectors–3x

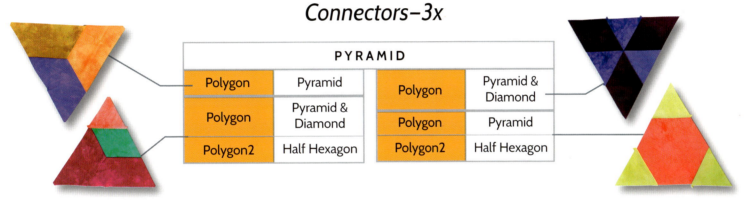

Connectors – 4x

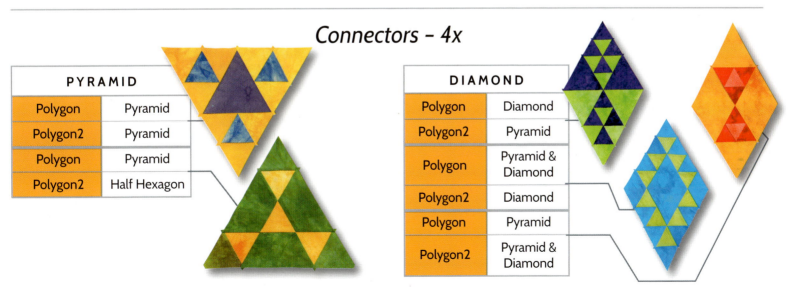

Young Love...Brian's Story

I remember the moment. It was 3rd grade. I sat bored, looking around for something more interesting than the class lesson. I scanned the room and saw a girl who mesmerized me. In youthful innocence and boldness, I mouthed the words, "I love you" when she looked over. I remember the sensation, a feeling of coming home, when I looked at her. Later, I desperately pleaded with (and convinced) my mom to drive me to Woolworth and, using my 8-year-old savings, bought that girl an engagement ring, presenting it on her birthday. I'm sure it was as elegant as a $10 ring could be.

The years took us in different directions but, curiously, our paths crossed periodically; we shared a college class, we performed in a theater production together, and once we passed on Ocean City's boardwalk. But each time I chickened out from talking with her. She married. I pursued my career. We followed our own separate life paths.

Luckily for me fate intervened again one night. We both, as it turns out, were members at a local gym. I normally would not have gone on this night but graduate school stress had taken its toll. I decided to work off some steam. I saw her as she waited for an aerobics class. I looked up her name on the gym sign-up sheet to be sure and convinced myself that enough was enough. This was the moment. The universe had found a big enough shoe to throw at my head to get the message though. I decided to talk to her. It was the best decision of my life.

Many moments, many years, and two children later, when I look at her I feel that same comfortable sensation of coming home. This year will be our 17th anniversary.

Brian and Kellie design together in their home graphic design studio.

Have a project? They'd love to hear from you. Contact them at brian.idesign@gmail.com and kellie.boehm@gmail.com or visit their website, idesigngraphicsonline.com

Love Eternal…Keziah's Diary

Love comes in many shapes and forms and, with love long-lasting, there is always a story.

At the mouth of the Susquehanna River in Darlington, Maryland sits Keziah's Diary. It's now a picturesque house sitting on a ridge overlooking miles of farmland, but it wasn't always this way.

Keziah's Diary was built circa 1810 by William Stump and later deeded to his daughter Keziah and her husband, Richard Jackson. Mr. Jackson was a businessman and an active community leader of his day. Keziah had a life like many prominent women of her time living south of the Mason-Dixie line. Stories were told throughout this Quaker farm town about the treatment of her slaves. Perhaps the truth of what really happened rests only in the pages of her diary.

The house eventually came into possession of George Robinson who owned the old Robinson Mill just north of Darlington. Time moved on and the landscape changed, but Keziah's Diary stood quietly defiant on her ridge.

Jeff and Kim Little have a passion for historic homes and were on a quest to find the perfect challenge. Kim's love matches her skill as an interior designer and home improvement contractor. Fearlessly, she removes generations of coatings and coverings to get to the base of plastered walls. In business for over twenty years, Kim works with clients to restore older homes, inside and out, to their original splendor.

Jeff's mission was to find a stone house for Kim to restore. That he did. Keziah's Diary had been neglected for over 50 years. It was overgrown with thickets and no longer visible from the road. Jeff and Kim purchased Keziah's Diary in 2006 and started the four-year journey of a major restoration to their field stone home. This included the original slave quarters and incorporated smokehouse, four chimneys, and original plaster walls. They retained the original millwork and handcrafted windows, wide pine floorboards, and a field stone icehouse. The garden walkways were sculpted from antique bricks salvaged from a nearby church. The front door still operates with the original 1810 key.

Kim's unending love paid off when Keziah's Diary was part of the 2009 Maryland House and Garden Pilgrimage. Keziah's Diary is listed on the National Register of Historic Places.

The beautiful photographs in this book were shot on location at Keziah's Diary.

Kim Little, designer
Greenwood Interiors
onefinehome@yahoo.com

Resources

It's not a quilt until it's finished. I used the expertise of professional longarm quilters to get my designs from the quilt studio to the *Polygon Affair*. Without them, the project would still be on the drawing board.

Beth Hanlon-Ridder has been an avid sewist all her life. Bit by the "Quilting Bug" in the early 90's, she bought a longarm machine and has been quilting for herself and others ever since. Beth has a real talent for knowing what quilting design works best on each quilt. You can find her at **bethridder.com** or on Facebook at **The Studio On Harvest Farm**.

Maria O'Haver is a longarm quilter who lives in Ellicott City, Maryland. Her favorite quote is from James Michener, slightly modified, that describes what she does.

"The master in the art of living makes little distinction between her work and her play. She hardly knows which is which. She simply pursues her vision of excellence at whatever she does, leaving others to decide whether she is working or playing. To her she's always doing both."

Maria's website is **mariaohaver.com** and she operates from Pangor Quilt Design Studio.

Ashley Malinowski started sewing when her mother took her to multiple summer camps from the age of six. By 12, Ashley got bit by the longarm bug because she was tired of always stitching in the ditch for her Delaware State Fair quilts. Then she discovered a longarm quilting machine rental program.

After using the machine several times, she headed to the Machine Quilting Expo (MQX) in Rhode Island her senior year of high school. She came home with a longarm to start her own business in June of 2010. Ever since, Ashley continues to longarm, both edge-to-edge designs and custom for customers and loves every minute of it.

Ashley can be reached through her website, **midnightquilter.weebly.com** and has a strong Facebook presence at **Midnight-Quilter**.

Peg Dougherty has been quilting in earnest since 1987 when her oldest daughter got married, but actually learned to quilt as a child with her mom. She has made over two hundred quilts and quilted projects. Her proudest moment came as a first place Hoffman Challenge winner for mixed technique.

Peg retired as a science teacher and school administrator in 2004. She has been longarm quilting since 2003. As a quilter, she likes to try new things. By allowing her creativity to flow, she never knows how her quilts are going to look when finished. She says, "They and I evolve!" Peg can be reached on line at **pegndavedou@wildblue.net**.

Acknowledgments

From the beginning, I believed that my journey in life wasn't just about me. While I know so many have touched my life and the outcome of *Polygon Affair*, it is with your love that I'm able to create and inspire.

First, I would like to thank Beth Hanlon-Ridder who has been an endearing friend since *Quilts: Unfinished Stories with New Endings*. Beth encouraged me to produce a large diamond tool that evolved into the **Polygon2 Tool**. She pushed me beyond my uncertainty to try a "modern" edge-to-edge quilting pattern for my beloved Butterflies quilt. Beth, thank you again and again for doing what you do and for being a valued friend.

Faith, the art of believing without seeing or having proof, is what some 90-plus quilters had when they participated in my online *Polygon Affair Mystery Series*. It was my first attempt at distance teaching and, through their patience, tolerance, and feedback I was able to design and produce four quilts for this book. However, it was their creative spirit that brings *Polygon Affair* to life by producing the quilts that appear in the galleries throughout the book. Thank you for staying connected.

"Lean on Me" song lyrics ring true when I think of Joyce Brown and Janice Edmonds-Scott. Through my tears and anxiety, stitch after stitch, they held strong in the belief that each day would be brighter for me if I stayed true to myself. With laughter and amusement, they encouraged the concept of *Polygon Affair* and indulged my chatter on how find my ultimate soulmate. Thank you for believing in me.

When I see the face of new love, young love, and devoted love, I smile. When *Polygon Affair* followed a love affair, I needed wedding photographs. The list is long of all the couples whose happiest day is now blazed within pages of *Polygon Affair*. Thank you for being the positive proof that love to marriage is worth the journey.

Blessed, that is the summary when you have talented friends like Peg Dougherty and Barbara Herron. Be it a thought or a rough sketch and jotted notes, quilts in my mind became a reality in their hands. Thank you for producing quilts for *Polygon Affair*. When I needed "modern" Mary Jo Yackley and Charlotte Noll responded. Wow! The simplicity and stunning machine quilting blew me away at first sight. Thank you for your vision.

Last, and far from least, thank you Mike McCarthy, Kim Little, Judy Wilson, Holly Kravec, and my love, Ray McGowan. You were the crew that brought *Polygon Affair* to life. It was a perfect early fall day. Kim's garden held the last blooms just long enough for the photo shoot. The creative spirit came together as each did what they do best. Special thanks to Holly the taskmaster who kept me on track to get this book to press while meeting the obligations of lecture and teaching venues.

The journey is tied to friends far and wide, new and forever, and loved ones close at hand. Thank you, all, for having faith, keeping me focused, and traveling with me on this journey through love. Thank you.

OUR *POLYGON AFFAIR* COUPLES

Alexandra and David	Dayna and Judah	Holly and Dennis	Kristen and Brian	Preston and Emily
Barbara and Bill	Elizabeth and Darren	Janna and Jeremy	Lane and Joe	Renee and Billy
Bob and Bobbi	Emily and Gabriel	Jeff and Linda	Laurence and Niki	Riquita and Michael
Brian and Heidi	Emma and Dean	Jennifer and Chris	Lena and Rodney	Sandy and Ed
Caroline and Marc	Erika and Chris	Josh and Tracey	Mary Lou and Melvin	Toni and Dennis
Chani and Cisco	Erin and Larry	Kaitlyn and Nicholas	Maxcine and Clifford	Tricia and Cliff
Chris and Vicky	Faheem and LaShana	Kata and Troy	Maxine and Billy	William and Tre'Sina
Chris and Evelyn	Gail and Carroll	Kaye and David	Megan and Eric	

Also Available

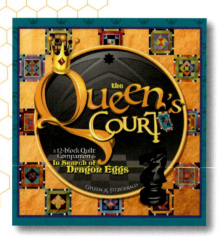

Coming Winter 2014

ISBN: 978-0-9768215-6-4

WITH PINEAPPLE TOOL

ISBN: 978-0-9768215-4-0

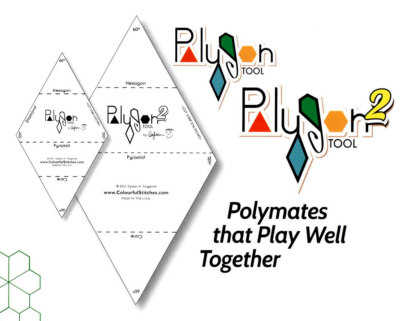

Polymates that Play Well Together

Quilts
Unfinished Stories with New Endings

ISBN: 978-0-9768215-0-2

LECTURES/WORKSHOPS

Gyleen is absolutely passionate about quilting and haiku poetry! Visit her on the web for patterns, note cards, and books, to schedule your group for her interactive lectures or workshops, or sign up for her free e-newsletter.

ORDERING INFORMATION

FPI Publishing books are available online or at your favorite bookstore.

FPI Publishing

For More Information, visit: **www.ColourfulStitches.com**

About the Author
Gyleen X. Fitzgerald

- SIGNATURE COLOR IS RED
- SEWING MACHINE OF CHOICE IS BERNINA 580
- GO TO THREAD IS AURIFIL 50WT COTTON
- LOVES THE WARMTH AND DRAPE OF LEGACY 100% COTTON BATTING
- BIG STITCHES WITH PRESENCIA #8 PERLE COTTON
- WOULD DIE FOR HOMEMADE POUND CAKE!

Gyleen Fitzgerald makes quilts that blend color, pattern and texture to provide a contemporary essence in traditional quilting. Her strength as a quilter is demonstrated by the infusion of engineering tools and innovative techniques to simplify visually complex quilts. She shares her enthusiasm for quilting through interactive lectures and workshops. As a writer, Gyleen centers on haiku poetry, quilt project books, magazine articles, and children's books.

An avid quilter, Gyleen has earned Best of Show honors and as a publisher, she is a Gold Medal winner for *Quilts: Unfinished Stories with New Endings*. She is best known for inspiring *Trash to Treasure Pineapple Quilts* and the creation of the **Pineapple Tool** *by Gyleen*.

Gyleen has appeared on *The Quilt Show* and *Lifetime TV* promoting a contemporary spirit in traditional quiltmaking.

For Gyleen, dreams hold no limits. Ray, her husband, is her shining light and quilting is her passion; together they color her world in a very special way.

Gyleen is a Philadelphia, Pennsylvania native who spent her formative years in Taiwan and Japan.